ILO Publications

Subscription Form 1981

To: **ILO Publications, International Labour Office, CH-1211 Geneva 22 (Switzerland)**

Please enter my order for 1981 for the publications ticked below, and invoice me accordingly.
(Please use BLOCK LETTERS) ☐ New ☐ Renewal (please check)

Full name:

Full address:

Country:

Date: Signature:

☐ I. **International Labour Review.** Articles on economic and social topics of international interest affecting labour, research notes, notices of new books received by the ILO. Six issues.
Annual subscription: Sw. Frs. 45; £11.25; $25.50. Price per number: Sw. Frs. 10; £2.50; $5.70.

☐ II. **Legislative Series.** Includes the most important national laws and regulations on labour and social security. Two main issues and index.
Annual subscription: Sw. Frs. 50; £12.50; $28.50. Price per number: Sw. Frs. 25; £6.25; $14.25.

☐ III. **Bulletin of Labour Statistics.** Articles on methodology and special topics. Trilingual tables of current statistics on employment, unemployment, wages, hours of work, consumer prices. (With updated supplements for intervening months.) Includes results of a detailed annual inquiry into wages, hours of work and consumer prices. Four main issues and eight supplements.
Annual subscription: Sw. Frs. 50; £12.50; $28.50. Price per main issue: Sw. Frs. 20; £5; $11.50.

☐ IV. **Year Book of Labour Statistics.** Trilingual. A comprehensive survey of annual data from all parts of the world relating to economically active population, employment, unemployment, hours of work, wages, industrial disputes, occupational injuries (most tables by industrial sectors) and consumer prices.
40th issue, 1980. Hard cover: Sw. Frs. 100; £25; $57.

☐ V. **Minutes of the Governing Body.** Normally published two or three times a year.
Annual subscription: Sw. Frs. 50; £12.50; $28.50.

☐ VI. **Official Bulletin. Series A:** Information on the activities of the ILO, texts adopted by the International Labour Conference and other official documents. Three issues. **Series B:** Reports of the Committee on Freedom of Association of the Governing Body of the ILO and related material. Two or three issues.
Annual subscription to Series A and B: Sw. Frs. 50; £12.50; $28.50. Price per number: Sw. Frs. 15; £3.75; $8.55.

☐ VII. **Social and Labour Bulletin.** Notes on current significant events, national and international, in the social and labour field; brief descriptions of major labour legislation, collective agreements, experiments in improving the work environment, etc. Four issues and index.
Annual subscription: Sw. Frs. 40; £10; $23. Price per issue: Sw. Frs. 12.50; £3.15; $7.15.

☐ VIII. **Labour Information Record.** A computer-operated data base containing full bibliographical references and short abstracts of all *Social and Labour Bulletin* articles, and citing major source material. Emphasis on: labour legislation; impact of new technologies; industrial relations; collective agreements; employment policies; quality of working life. Three issues.
Annual subscription: Sw. Frs. 30; £7.50; $17. Price per issue: Sw. Frs. 10; £2.50; $5.70.

☐ IX. **International Labour Documentation.** A bibliographical record based on current acquisitions in the ILO Central Library, covering the fields of industrial relations, management, manpower planning, vocational training and other problems of economics and social development. Twelve issues containing short abstracts of all titles listed.
Annual subscription: Sw. Frs. 60; £15; $34. Price per issue: Sw. Frs. 10; £2.50; $5.70.

☐ X. **Documents of the International Labour Conference.** Reports prepared for each item on the agenda of the annual Conference and the Record of Proceedings. Sixteen to 18 volumes.
Annual subscription: Sw. Frs. 280; £70; $160. Individual reports at varying prices.

- ☐ XI. **Women at Work.** A news bulletin exclusively devoted to questions concerning the economic and social contribution of women to society. Two issues.
Annual subscription: Sw. Frs. 20; £5; $11.50. Price per issue: Sw. Frs. 12.50; £3.15; $7.15.

- ☐ XII. **Judgments of the Administrative Tribunal of the ILO.** Two issues.
Annual subscription: Sw. Frs. 40; £10; $23. Separate issues at varying prices.

- ☐ XIII. **Labour Education.** Designed to promote the educational activities of trade union organisations and other workers' education bodies. Three issues.
Annual subscription: Sw. Frs. 30; £7.50; $17. Price per issue: Sw. Frs. 12.50; £3.15; $7.15.

- ☐ XIV. **Documents of the Regional Conferences.** Reports to the four ILO Regional Conferences, covering Africa, the Americas, Asia and Europe.
Individual reports at varying prices.

- ☐ XV. **Documents of Industrial Meetings.** The main reports prepared for industrial committees and analogous and other industrial meetings, as well as notes on the proceedings of certain meetings.
Individual reports at varying prices.

- ☐ XVI. **Labour-Management Relations Series.** Occasional monographs and reports on labour laws and labour-management relations.
Issued at varying prices.

- ☐ XVII. **Management Development Series.** Occasional monographs dealing with specialised management subjects and management development methods.
Issued at varying prices.

- ☐ XVIII. **The Cost of Social Security.** A world-wide comparison of social security expenditures.
Issued every three years at varying prices.

- ☐ XIX. **Occupational Safety and Health Series.** Occasional technical monographs and reports on occupational health and safety protection against sickness, disease and injury.
Issued at varying prices.

- ☐ XX. **WEP Studies.** A collection of manuals, studies, monographs and reports issued under the ILO World Employment Programme (WEP), whose principal objective is to help eradicate mass poverty and unemployment.
Issued at varying prices.

- ☐ XXI. **Special Publications.** Miscellaneous non-serial sales publications on a wide range of subjects not comprised in any of the above groups. They include the following: codes of practice and illustrated guides on safety and health; major reference works and international comparative studies; research monographs and reports on particular countries or issues; specialised bibliographies and directories; training and workers' education material; specialised statistical handbooks.
Issued at varying prices.

Combined subscriptions are offered at special **reduced rates** for certain publications, as follows:

☐	Subscription C/O: Items VII and VIII	(save 30%)	Sw. Frs. 49;	£12.25;	$28
☐	Subscription C/A: Items I, VI, VII and VIII	(save 30%)	Sw. Frs. 115.50;	£29;	$66
☐	Subscription C/B: Items III and IV	(save 20%)	Sw. Frs. 120;	£30;	$68.50
☐	Subscription C/C: Items I to XI	(save 40%)	Sw. Frs. 465;	£116.25;	$265
☐	Subscription C/D: Items I to XIX	(save approx. 45%)	Sw. Frs. 670;	£167.50;	$382

Standing orders may also be placed for the publications listed under items XIV to XXI.

The prices indicated cover one calendar year (1 January to 31 December) and include postage by surface mail. Air mail and registered mail charges are extra. Subscriptions and standing orders cover new publications and revised editions; they exclude reimpressions and reissues of previously published material.
The £ sterling rates apply in the UK and the $ rates in the US only. In all other countries it is the local currency equivalent of the Swiss franc rates that is payable.
Orders may be placed through major booksellers, subscription agencies or ILO local offices in many countries or sent direct to ILO Publications, International Labour Office, CH-1211 Geneva 22, Switzerland.

ISSN 0020-7780

International Labour Review 1980

Volume 119 Number 6 NOVEMBER-DECEMBER

Contents

Articles appearing in the *International Labour Review* are indexed and abstracted in the *Journal of Economic Literature* (Nashville (Tennessee)), the *Public Affairs Information Service Bulletin* (New York) and *Personnel Management Abstracts* (Ann Arbor (Michigan)). Whole collections and back numbers of the *International Labour Review* in microform, as well as photocopies of separate articles, are obtainable from University Microfilms International, 300 North Zeeb Road, Ann Arbor, Michigan 48106 (United States), and 18 Bedford Row, London WC1R 4EJ (England).

International Labour Review, Vol. 119, No. 6, November-December 1980

The 66th Session of the International Labour Conference, June 1980

The 66th Session of the International Labour Conference was held in Geneva from 4 to 25 June 1980 and was attended by delegations from 138 member States. The United States of America, after an absence of two years, and Lesotho, which had withdrawn from the ILO in 1971, resumed their places among the member States, whose ranks were further swelled by Grenada, the Socialist Republic of Viet Nam and St. Lucia. Zimbabwe, present to begin with as an observer, was admitted as a Member of the ILO on 6 June, the date on which its delegation accordingly took its place in the hall. Observers were present from Antigua, Belize, Bermuda and the Holy See, as were representatives of numerous international organisations, both governmental and non-governmental, and other bodies invited by the Conference.

In addition to the annual report of the Director-General (which, following a first part devoted to training, dealt with the activities of the ILO in 1979 and included appendices describing the action taken on earlier Conference resolutions and presenting a new report on the position of workers of the occupied Arab territories), a report submitted by the Governing Body summarising the more important decisions it had taken since the 65th Session, the regular report on the application of international labour Conventions and Recommendations, a number of financial and administrative questions, the sixteenth special report on apartheid and the report of the working party set up to consider the structure of the ILO, the Conference had before it four technical items. These concerned (1) older workers: work and retirement; (2) promotion of collective bargaining; (3) equal opportunities and equal treatment for men and women workers: workers with family responsibilities; and (4) safety and health and the working environment, and amendment of the list of occupational diseases appended to the Employment Injury Benefits Convention, 1964 (No. 121).

The Conference adopted a Recommendation on the first item. It held a first discussion on the three other items with a view to adopting international instruments at next year's session and amended the list of occupational diseases appended to Convention No. 121. It reviewed the progress made by the Working Party on Structure and decided to extend its mandate so that it could report on the final results of its work at the 67th Session of the Conference. It adopted the report and conclusions of the Committee on Apartheid. In regard to the budget it decided that the United States' contribution for 1980 should be used to cover a cash deficit, while that for 1981, fixed at 25 per cent of the income, would enable the contributions of the other member States to be proportionally reduced. In addition, it authorised the provision of up to US$4.5 million to pay off outstanding liabilities of the International Centre for Advanced Technical and Vocational Training in Turin.[1]

A special sitting was held on 17 June on the occasion of the visit of Mr. Constantin Caramanlis. The President of the Hellenic Republic stressed, amongst other things, that in the face of the complex and dangerous problems of inflation, unemployment, the energy crisis and the inequality between North and South, the international community should concentrate attention on two major objectives: "the consolidation of world peace and the prosperity of mankind within the framework of a new international order, which would strengthen the role of labour and in due course make work more human". On 19 June it was Mr. Willy Brandt, Nobel Peace Prize winner, who was the guest of honour of the Conference. In his capacity as Chairman of the Independent Commission on International Development Issues, he presented the programme which this Commission has described as a Programme for Survival and which calls for four major objectives to be achieved during the next five years: a greater transfer of resources, an agreed international energy strategy and an assured global supply of energy, the elimination of mass hunger, and structural reforms in international organisations and in institutions which influence the world's economic system. Efforts to ensure the survival of the human race should be based on the growing interdependence between States and regions and on the realisation that North-South relations transcend the mere economic dimension. Hence the importance of the role played by social organisations such as the ILO.

The following sections of this article deal in turn with the Conference's discussion of the four technical items on its agenda, the application of the Declaration concerning the Policy of Apartheid, its annual review of the implementation of Conventions and Recommendations, and the three resolutions it adopted on questions not included in its agenda. In conclusion, a brief account is given of the debate on the report of the Director-General as well as of his reply.

Older workers: work and retirement

Following the first discussion of this item at the 65th Session of the Conference,[2] the Office had prepared—on the basis of the Conclusions adopted and the comments received from governments—two reports containing the text of a proposed Recommendation.[3] Since the majority of governments had once again declared themselves in favour of adopting only a Recommendation, it had not been possible to meet the request of the Workers' members and some Government members made during the first discussion that a draft Convention should also be prepared.

As had happened the year before, the Committee on Older Workers set up by the Conference immediately came up against a strong divergence of opinion between, on the one hand, the Workers' members and some Governments who argued for a framework Convention laying down a number of fundamental principles supplemented by a detailed Recommendation and, on the other hand, the Employers' members and some other Governments who advocated the adoption of a single instrument—a Recommendation—sufficiently flexible to take account of differing national situations. Following a thorough discussion the Workers formally proposed that the Committee should also examine a draft Convention, but this proposal was finally rejected and the Committee decided to proceed with the preparation of a Recommendation only.

With a view to making the instrument more flexible and comprehensive, the Committee suggested a number of amendments to the text prepared by the Office regarding, in particular, the means of implementing the policy of equality of opportunity and treatment for which it called, and the right of workers to give their views on the new employment opportunities offered. It also proposed introducing some new elements such as studies to identify types of activity likely to hasten the ageing process, the participation of employers' and workers' organisations in the process of adapting systems of remuneration, assistance in securing new employment, facilitating the access of older persons to the employment market, and the content of retirement preparation programmes.

The Conference unanimously adopted the Recommendation concerning older workers. This instrument, which comprises 33 Paragraphs, applies to all workers "who are liable to encounter difficulties in employment and occupation because of advancement in age": the competent authority of each country may adopt more precise definitions. It is understood that these problems should be dealt with in the context of national employment policy and a social policy designed to ensure that employment problems are not merely shifted from one group of workers to another.

The Recommendation lays down guidelines covering all aspects of the conditions of employment and work of older workers, for whom the member States are invited to formulate and implement an appropriate policy in three main fields: equality of opportunity and treatment, protection in employment, and preparation for and access to retirement.

First of all it is provided (Para. 3) that measures should be taken for the prevention of discrimination in the various areas of working life enumerated in Paragraph 5. For the implementation of this policy, which should involve the effective participation of employers' and workers' organisations, it is recommended that legislation be enacted and programmes of action promoted, that existing provisions should be examined and where necessary adapted, that observance of the policy be enforced in all activities under the direction or control of a public authority and promoted in the other sectors, and that all the persons and organisations concerned should have access to the bodies empowered to examine and investigate complaints.

Secondly it is recommended (Para. 11) that measures be devised, again with the participation of employers' and workers' organisations, to enable older workers to continue in employment under satisfactory conditions. Studies on this subject should first be undertaken and their findings widely disseminated. Next, solutions must be sought to the difficulties encountered by older workers in respect of adaptation, particularly as regards certain conditions of work and of the working environment, the organisation of work in general and of particular jobs, different arrangements of working time, systems of remuneration, safety and health, and vocational guidance and training. In addition, measures might be taken to make alternative employment opportunities available to those older workers desiring them, and special efforts should be made to help older workers who are affected by workforce reductions or are seeking employment after having been kept out of the workforce by their family responsibilities.

Thirdly it is recommended, in the interests of a gradual transition from working life to retirement, that measures should be taken wherever possible to ensure that the cessation of gainful activity is voluntary and that the age at which old-age pensions are payable should be made flexible (Para. 21). To this end, provisions making mandatory the termination of employment at a specified age should be examined and older workers who are fit for work should be able to defer their claim to an old-age benefit, a special compensatory benefit should be granted to older workers whose hours of work are reduced, resources should be guaranteed for older persons who have been out of work for a lengthy period, and early retirement benefits should be payable to older workers who are engaged in arduous or unhealthy occupations, who are recognised as being unfit for work, or who wish to retire early for reasons of personal convenience subject to reductions in the level of their old-age pension. In addition, retirement preparation programmes should provide information in a wide variety of fields.

Finally, measures should be taken to ensure that all concerned—individuals, services and organisations—are informed of the problems which older people encounter and of the proposed solutions.

Promotion of collective bargaining

Although the practice of collective bargaining has expanded considerably in the past three decades its development continues to run up against various difficulties. In a number of countries there are still in fact legal restrictions which are likely to affect its scope, content or procedures. Moreover, the percentage of workers covered and the range of negotiable issues still vary greatly from one country to another and, within countries, according to the branch of activity and category of worker. In addition, it is sometimes handicapped by the absence or inadequacy of rules governing the way it should be carried out. The development of collective bargaining can also be held back when, as is now often the case, it has to be conducted against a difficult economic background of inflation, unemployment or underdevelopment. It may be particularly difficult in such situations to preserve the voluntary nature of collective bargaining since in some countries the public authorities tend to intervene to ensure that the negotiators do not jeopardise the general interest.

For some 30 years the ILO has been very active in promoting collective bargaining through, for example, the publication of studies and the organisation of meetings. On the other hand, it must be noted that the Conference has adopted comparatively few standards on the subject. The most important are Article 4 of the Right to Organise and Collective Bargaining Convention, 1949 (No. 98), and the Collective Agreements Recommendation, 1951 (No. 91). It was with a view to supplementing these standards, whose principal aim is to recognise the *right* to bargain collectively, that the Governing Body decided to place on the agenda of the 66th Session of the Conference an item entitled "Promotion of collective bargaining", for which the Office, in accordance with its normal procedure, prepared two reports as a basis for the first discussion.[4]

The Conclusions adopted by the Conference first of all recall the key importance of existing international standards on the subject and state that, without revising them, the new standards designed to promote collective bargaining should give greater effect to their objectives.

According to the Conclusions, the term "collective bargaining" should extend to all negotiations conducted for the purpose of determining working conditions and terms of employment or regulating relations between employers and workers or their organisations.

The central Point of the Conclusions provides that measures should be taken to ensure that *(a)* collective bargaining is made possible for all employers and all groups of workers in the branches of activity covered by the new standards; *(b)* collective bargaining is progressively extended to all matters concerning working conditions and terms of employment as well as relations between employers and workers or their organisations; *(c)* collective bargaining is not hampered by the absence of rules governing the procedure to be used or by the inadequacy or inappropriateness of such rules; and *(d)* bodies and procedures for the settlement of labour disputes are so conceived as to contribute to the promotion of collective bargaining. According to the same Point, such measures may not be so interpreted or applied as to hamper the freedom of collective bargaining.

The Conclusions go on to list a number of specific means that could be employed relating, inter alia, to the establishment and growth, on a voluntary basis, of free, independent and representative employers' and workers' organisations; the recognition of such organisations for the purposes of collective bargaining; the training of negotiators; the granting to negotiators of the necessary mandate to conduct and conclude negotiations; and giving the parties access to the information required for meaningful negotiations. Elsewhere the Conclusions state that collective bargaining should be possible at any level, including that of the establishment, the undertaking or the branch of activity, and that where it takes place at several levels the parties should seek to ensure that there is co-ordination among these levels.

It was the scope of the new standards and the form of the instrument(s) that led to the toughest discussions.

As regards the scope, it is provided that the new standards should, "subject to national laws, regulations and practice, apply to all branches of economic activity". It has been argued that this text, which was adopted by a very small majority during the work in committee, makes it possible for member States to fix the scope as they wish, whereas the text proposed by the Office only enabled them to exclude from its scope certain groups of persons employed by public authorities.

As regards the form of the instrument to be adopted there was wide agreement that only the adoption of a Recommendation should be proposed, whereas the Office had suggested the adoption of a Convention supplemented by a Recommendation. The arguments developed on this point by the Employers and Workers were nevertheless very different. The Employers wanted a Recommendation, and only that, for reasons of flexibility. The Workers, for their part, would have preferred a Convention supplemented by a Recommendation but they finally voted for the adoption of a single instrument—a Recommendation—since the text of the Conclusions did not in their view represent a sufficient advance on the existing standards to justify a new Convention on the subject. They considered, in particular, that the Conclusions left the member States too much freedom to determine the scope of the proposed standards. They declared that their objective would still be to strengthen the text of the Conclusions during the second discussion in 1981 in such a way as to make it possible to adopt a Convention supplemented by a Recommendation.

There were also major differences in two other areas between the Conclusions proposed by the Office and those the Conference adopted.

First, the Conclusions proposed by the Office contained a provision whereby measures should be taken "to encourage and facilitate reconciling the specific interests of the parties to collective bargaining with the general interest". This Point was deleted during the discussion. Many members of the Committee, while recognising that the problem was a real one, considered that it was so delicate and raised so many difficulties—

especially with respect to definition—that it would be better not to deal with it in the Conclusions.

Secondly, the Office text contained a provision whereby measures should be taken "so that the parties negotiate in good faith and refrain from any practices that are liable to hamper the collective bargaining process". This Point was also deleted in the course of the discussion, mainly because the Workers and a number of Governments considered that the concepts involved could not be defined sufficiently precisely.

Equal opportunities and equal treatment for men and women workers: workers with family responsibilities

The Conference held a first discussion of this item. The Governing Body, in deciding at its November 1978 Session to place the question on the Conference agenda, had sought to take the ILO's standard-setting activity a step further on the path towards complete equality of opportunity and treatment for men and women workers in employment and occupation.

Some Governments, particularly those of the Scandinavian countries, would have liked the Conference to deal with the whole question of equal opportunities and equal treatment for workers of both sexes, instead of restricting its focus to the problems of workers with family responsibilities. They nevertheless recognised that the difficulty of combining occupational and family responsibilities was a major obstacle in the way of achieving equal opportunities and equal treatment. This was partly because family responsibilities often act as a powerful brake on the effective exercise of the right to work, and partly because measures to combat discrimination in training, access to employment and working conditions often have only a limited effect if, because of these responsibilities, some workers have to give up their job or normal advancement in their careers.

Almost all the members of the Committee set up by the Conference to discuss this item[5] agreed that it was opportune, and indeed most desirable, to adopt new standards on equality of opportunity and treatment for men and women workers with family responsibilities. Some Government members from developing countries stressed, however, that action in this area was not perhaps uppermost among the priorities of countries faced with problems of unemployment and underemployment, where there was still much to be done to eliminate poverty, illiteracy and disease, and where, in some cases, the concept of equality between men and women might clash with traditional attitudes or religious beliefs.

When it adopted, in 1975, the Declaration on Equality of Opportunity and Treatment for Women Workers,[6] the Conference had recognised that the position of women could not be changed unless there was a corresponding change in the role of men within the family. It was now becoming increasingly clear, and the discussions of the Committee confirmed this awareness, that the attainment of equality in working life is to a large extent dependent on that of equality within the family. It was not surprising, therefore, that the Conclusions adopted by the Committee were based on a dual concern: on the one hand, to promote the idea that men and women should share family responsibilities equally, this being a precondition for the attainment of equality of opportunity and treatment in working life, and, on the other hand, to give men and women workers with family responsibilities effective equality of opportunity and treatment with other workers.

It was only following a lengthy discussion that the Committee arrived at its decision regarding the form the proposed new standards should take. Those advocating that only a Recommendation should be adopted argued that, since it was impossible to foresee the legal, social and economic consequences of the measures envisaged, a circumspect approach was indicated; they underlined the great diversity of ways in which the problems under consideration are being tackled in the different countries as a result of the marked influence of economic, social and cultural conditions and hence the wide variety of solutions it was possible to reach. The advocates of a Convention supplemented by a Recommendation, whose point of view prevailed, pointed to the magnitude of the problem and the need for member States to adopt a voluntarist approach which alone was capable of creating the necessary economic and social conditions for its solution.

The definition of the concept of family responsibilities also gave rise to prolonged discussion. All the members were agreed in considering that it should be defined precisely so as to limit the scope of the proposed standards to workers who are genuinely placed at a disadvantage because of such responsibilities. While it was easy to specify, in regard to responsibilities in respect of children, that they should be taken into consideration only in relation to the dependent children of workers, a number of proposals were put forward regarding other members of the family. It was decided that the proposed standards should—by stages if necessary—apply to men and women workers with responsibilities in relation to other members of their immediate family who clearly need their care or support.

The Conclusions proposed by the Committee, which will serve as a basis for the discussion at next year's session of the Conference, contain provisions concerning the objectives of national policy, training and employment, terms and conditions of employment, child-care and family services and facilities, social security, and help in the exercise of family responsibilities.

Safety and health and the working environment

Recent years have brought a growing conviction of the need to replace ad hoc, piecemeal action on occupational hazards by a more systematic, comprehensive approach. The case for a shift of this sort was set out in a report[7] drawn up by the Office to prepare the way for consideration of this agenda item by the Conference. The report concluded with a questionnaire in which governments were invited to give their views on whether an international instrument (or instruments) on the subject should be adopted and, if so, what ground it should cover. The replies received from 63 member States showed a majority preference for a Convention supplemented by a Recommendation, and a second report,[7] after summarising the views expressed, put forward suggestions regarding the content of the proposed instruments. These formed the basis for the work of the Committee set up by the Conference to consider the matter during the first stage of the double-discussion procedure.

The proposals before the Committee covered the entire question of the prevention of occupational hazards and the improvement of the working environment. Their purpose, in the words of the representative of the Secretary-General, was "to lay the foundations for a national policy within each member State to establish as far as possible a total and coherent system of prevention, taking into consideration the present-day realities of the working world". These proposals did not necessarily call for immediate action; they were intended above all to encourage member States to promote the progressive application of new and far-reaching measures at the national and enterprise levels.

Opening the general discussion the Chairman of the Committee expressed her firm conviction that, regardless of the differences between the social systems of member countries and between the levels of technology they used, from the point of view of safety and health and the working environment all countries were developing ones.

The Employers believed that favourable results at the workplace could best be achieved by co-operation, and that legislation had limited effect unless it enjoyed the support of both workers and employers. Their experience was that the elaboration of legal requirements in this field could sometimes erode the employer's clear responsibility for safety and health matters and thus reduce protection for workers rather than improve it. In their view the aim should be to adopt instruments which could be widely ratified, bearing in mind the diversity of national legal and industrial relations systems.

The Workers' members felt that despite the differences in the levels of social and economic development in member States the instruments should have a full legal basis in all countries and should apply to all workers in all sectors. In particular, they insisted, those working in the public service should be included, and the definition clause was amended in this sense.

The meaning of the word "health" gave rise to a good deal of discussion. The Workers' and some Government members wanted to see it extended beyond the traditional sense of absence of disease. The words "well-being" were added but this amendment encountered opposition in the Committee and later in the plenary sitting of the Conference. Next year's Session will be taking a second look at the phrase "occupational health including well-being" to see if another, more descriptive form of wording can be found.

Other matters which elicited some debate concerned the degree of consultation that should take place between governments and the representative organisations of employers and workers when drawing up national legislation in this field, and the worker's right to cease work if he judges it to involve immediate and serious danger to his life or health.

Some indication of the comprehensive nature of the texts ultimately agreed on by the Committee may be had from just a few extracts taken from the proposed conclusions with a view to the adoption of a Convention. The "coherent national policy" required of ratifying member States should, it was agreed, cover the design, testing, integration, choice, substitution, installation, arrangement, use and maintenance of machinery and equipment, substances and chemical, physical and biological agents used, and work processes; the adaptation of machinery, equipment, working time, organisation of work and work processes to the physical and mental capacities of the workers; the training, retraining, qualifications and motivation of persons involved in the achievement of adequate levels of safety and health; and communication and co-operation at the levels of the work group and the undertaking as well as at the national level.

Action called for at the national level includes the institution of an appropriate system of inspection to enforce occupational safety and health laws and regulations, with adequate penalties for violations; and guidance to help employers and workers comply with their legal obligations. The competent authorities should progressively assume responsibility for determining the conditions governing the construction and lay-out of undertakings and major alterations affecting them, prohibiting or limiting the use of hazardous substances, establishing procedures for the notification of occupational accidents and diseases and for the production of annual statistics, and holding inquiries into serious accidents or diseases. There follow requirements regarding the design, manufacture and sale of machinery, equipment and substances to ensure proper standards and safe use, as well as the inclusion of safety and health questions at all levels of education and training.

Further provisions relate to action that is called for at the level of the factory or plant, and to a good deal more which lack of space prevents describing here. The text of the proposed supplementary Recommendation goes into even greater detail.

The Committee's report was approved by the Conference in plenary sitting without opposition. The discussion will be resumed at the 67th Session of the Conference next year.

Amendment of the list of occupational diseases appended to the Employment Injury Benefits Convention, 1964 (No. 121)

When it adopted the Employment Injury Benefits Convention (No. 121) in 1964 the Conference, recognising that the schedule of occupational diseases giving entitlement to benefit would have to be kept up to date, requested the Governing Body to convene a meeting of experts charged with preparing "a draft list of occupational diseases which would take account of all recent information on the subject", and to include the revision of this list in the agenda of a future session of the Conference. The same request was repeated by the Conference in 1967 and 1970.

The updating of the list was made necessary by the discovery of new cause-effect relationships between physical, chemical or biological agents in the working environment and the state of health of the worker. In addition to facilitating the harmonisation of social security benefits at the international level, updating and extending the list could help to prevent occupational diseases by promoting a greater knowledge of hazards and encouraging medical supervision of workers and control measures for harmful agents.

A meeting of experts, organised by the ILO in co-operation with the WHO in January 1980, was therefore asked "to set criteria for determining the list of occupational diseases and, in the light of the most up-to-date medical and technical knowledge, to draft a new list of diseases, which would be submitted to the Conference for consideration".[8]

Only three diseases were included in the schedule of the Workmen's Compensation (Occupational Diseases) Convention, 1925 (No. 18); ten in that of Convention No. 42 of 1934, which revised the earlier one; and 15 in the schedule of Convention No. 121, which superseded the two preceding instruments. This year the experts' proposal included 29 occupational diseases.

The Conference accepted the validity of the criteria adopted by the meeting of experts for selection of the occupational diseases to be included in the new list. Since this list could not give a detailed definition of the diseases in question nor of the working conditions likely to give rise to them, the Conference considered that it would be necessary to establish practical directives, criteria, examples or instructions for its use but that this was essentially a matter for the competent national authority. In addition, to draw attention to the qualitative and quantitative aspects of exposure to health hazards, it decided to indicate in a footnote to the list that in the application of the schedule the degree and type of exposure should be taken into account when appropriate.

The Conference made only slight changes to the proposals submitted by the experts and it adopted the new list of occupational diseases by 424 votes in favour and none against, with 9 abstentions.[9]

The Conference also noted the comments of the meeting of experts concerning a number of other hazards apt to give rise to diseases which might later be considered for inclusion in the list of occupational diseases: these observations warranted the attention of the ILO and WHO in their work relating to occupational diseases. It considered, finally, that the list and appropriate guidelines for its practical use should be periodically revised in the light of technical progress and new scientific knowledge.

Implementation of the Declaration concerning the Policy of Apartheid of the Republic of South Africa (1964)

With a view to finding practical ways of strengthening the ILO's contribution to the elimination of apartheid, the Governing Body had organised a tripartite meeting on the subject shortly before the 66th Session of the Conference. The purpose of the meeting was to analyse the changes which have been proposed or made in apartheid as regards labour matters in the Republic of South Africa, to evaluate present ILO activities in this field and to explore other forms of action. A great many suggestions had been made at the meeting, whose report was submitted to the Conference as an addendum to the special report of the Director-General on apartheid. In accordance with a recommendation made by the Governing Body, the Conference set up for the first time a Committee on Apartheid, which had before it the two above-mentioned reports.

The general discussion in the Committee revealed that there was unanimity regarding the objective to be pursued—the eradication of apartheid—but that agreement still had to be reached on the most effective means of attaining it. The Workers' members had drafted a paper listing the proposals they wished to see discussed and adopted. Supplemented subsequently by proposals presented by the Employers' and some Government members, this paper eventually resulted in the adoption of a number of recommendations concerning: (1) government action through the United Nations; (2) government action; (3) action by employers' organisations; (4) action of trade unions the world over; and (5) ILO action.

It should be noted that there was unanimity on all the points relating to ILO action. Amongst other things, the Organisation is invited to update the 1964 Declaration concerning the Policy of Apartheid and to set up tripartite machinery to carry out annual monitoring of the action taken in this connection by governments, employers and workers. The ILO should also expand its activities relating to the diffusion of information as well as those it undertakes in the field of education, workers' education and management training and its technical assistance to the liberation movements, Black workers and their independent trade unions in South Africa. It is also invited to encourage and extend financial support to workers' and employers' organisations in their programmes of action against apartheid. Finally, it is called upon to co-operate closely with the Organisation of African Unity, the United Nations Special Committee against Apartheid and, in general, with the United Nations and its specialised agencies in order to intensify and co-ordinate all activities whose ultimate objective is to eliminate apartheid in all its facets. In particular it should organise, before the 1981 Session of the Conference, an international tripartite meeting in one of the "front-line" States to plan a joint programme of action.

Governments, for their part, are invited to give effect to the relevant resolutions of the United Nations, which include, for example, an embargo on deliveries of arms and oil to the Republic; they should also sever all relations with South Africa, stop public and private investment there, discourage emigration and tourism to the country, withhold recognition of the "Bantustans" and increase their support for independent African States enclaved within or immediately neighbouring the Republic of South Africa, as well as for the liberation movements.

Employers' organisations are called upon to ensure that their members do not maintain relations with the Pretoria regime and that economic and financial groups do not extend loans to it; foreign companies are also requested to withdraw their investments and to refrain from any co-operation with South Africa in the economic and military fields.

The recommendations invite trade unions to put pressure, including recourse to industrial action, on companies investing in South Africa which do not recognise African trade unions; to mobilise the rank-and-file in solidarity action with the workers of South Africa; to give financial and moral support to the African trade unions and to insist on compliance with the codes of conduct adopted for companies investing in South Africa.

The action proposed for governments and employers was the subject of a number of reservations, certain governments and employers considering that some of the proposed measures did not come within the competence of the ILO or risked harming the very people they were intended to help.

The Conference devoted two plenary sitting to the discussion of the report of the Committee on Apartheid. At the end of this debate, which provided an opportunity to discuss the latest developments in the Republic of South Africa in the field of labour in general and, in particular, to shed light on the extremely difficult situation facing the Black trade union movement, the Conference endorsed the report and conclusions of the Committee.

Application of Conventions and Recommendations

As it does each year, the Conference Committee on the Application of Conventions and Recommendations reviewed the measures taken by the member States to fulfil their obligations under the ILO Constitution with respect to international labour standards and, in particular, the application of Conventions they have ratified. The Committee once again took as the basis for its work the report of the Committee of Experts on the Application of Conventions and Recommendations; appreciation for the high quality of this report was expressed by the spokesmen of the Workers' and Employers' members and a large number of Government members, who paid tribute to the independence, objectivity and impartiality with which the Committee of Experts had performed its difficult task.

The Conference Committee devoted considerable attention to an examination of its own working methods and the basic principles governing its supervision of the application of ratified Conventions. At the 1979 Session of the Conference the Committee had established a tripartite working party to examine what changes, if any, might be made in its methods of work as regards the "special list" and "special paragraphs" in its report, the aim of which is to draw the Conference's attention to the serious difficulties which some States appear to have in fulfilling their obligations. The working party had not been able, in the time available to it, to reach specific conclusions. Accordingly the Committee decided to establish another working party at the current session of the Conference to re-examine the question in the light of the results achieved last year and of the comments and suggestions received in the meantime from governments and employers' and workers' organisations.

On the proposal of this working party, the Committee decided that its report should henceforth contain a section entitled "Application of ratified Conventions", in which it will draw the attention of the Conference to cases of progress, certain special cases, and cases of continued failure to apply Conventions. In addition, various types of failure to provide information (previously enumerated under criteria 1 to 6 of the special list) will be presented in narrative form in separate paragraphs at the end of each of the appropriate sections of the report. In the future the Committee will also include in its report a paragraph noting any cases of failure for the past three years to indicate the organisations of employers and workers to which copies of reports and information supplied to the ILO under articles 19 and 22 of the Constitution have been communicated in accordance with article 23 (2).

In this connection the Committee emphasised the important contribution that employers' and workers' organisations can make to the better application of international labour standards.

The major part of the Committee's work was devoted to discussing with representatives of the countries concerned problems arising in connection with the application of ratified Conventions or compliance with the obligation to submit reports or other obligations laid down in the ILO Constitution. The Committee received information from 38 governments. With two exceptions all the countries which were named in connection with the examination of individual cases and were represented at the Conference availed themselves of the opportunity to state their position.

The Committee noted with satisfaction the continuing efforts made by governments to ensure compliance with ratified Conventions. It was pleased to learn that the Committee of Experts had noted 73 cases in which governments had made the necessary changes in their law and practice following observations by that Committee. This brought the number of cases of progress noted by the Committee of Experts to more than 1,300 since it began to list them in 1964.

The Committee drew the Conference's attention to the discussions it had held on some special cases. It expressed its concern about the application of certain Conventions by six States and welcomed the information supplied by one government regarding progress made in the application of the Forced Labour Convention, 1930 (No. 29).

This year the Committee did not list any case of continued failure to eliminate serious deficiencies in the application of ratified Conventions.

There was a broad measure of agreement in the Committee as to the usefulness of the direct contacts procedure established in 1969. Under this procedure a representative of the ILO Director-General may visit the country concerned, with the agreement of the government, in a joint endeavour to overcome the difficulties encountered and clear up any uncertainties or misunderstandings. The Committee noted that direct contacts had taken place recently in several countries and that new requests for contacts had been received while the Conference was in session. The recent appointment by the ILO of three regional advisers on international labour standards was welcomed by the Workers' members and several Government members.

The Committee noted with satisfaction that 114 ratifications had been registered during the past 12 months; this brought the total number of ratifications to more than 4,800. The steady rate at which governments of industrialised and developing countries alike continued to ratify bore witness to their constant attachment to the ILO's standard-setting work.

The Employers' and Workers' members, as well as several Government members, welcomed the Governing Body's decision to request special reports at four-yearly intervals from States not yet having ratified the Discrimination (Employment and Occupation) Convention, 1958 (No. 111). The Committee stressed the particular importance of this instrument and expressed the hope that the new reporting procedure would encourage governments to take the necessary measures to overcome existing obstacles to ratification. Given the flexibility of the Convention, few governments ought to experience serious difficulties in ratifying and implementing it.

The Committee also discussed the general survey on migrant workers made by the Committee of Experts on the basis of reports concerning the application of the Migration for Employment Convention (Revised), 1949 (No. 97), the Migration for Employment Recommendation (Revised), 1949 (No. 86), the Migrant Workers (Supplementary Provisions) Convention,

1975 (No. 143), and the Migrant Workers Recommendation, 1975 (No. 151). In conclusion, it emphasised the importance of the Conventions on migrant workers and expressed the hope that the general survey would help governments to overcome difficulties in their ratification and application. Continuing action was necessary to resolve the problems of migrant workers, and the ILO, with its long tripartite experience in this field, should participate actively in the work being undertaken in the United Nations for their protection. The question of further ILO measures should be considered in due course in the light of the results of the United Nations initiative and of developments in the world situation.

The Committee's report was adopted by the Conference in plenary sitting.

Resolutions on questions not included in the agenda of the Conference

The Conference adopted three resolutions on various questions not included in its agenda.

The first—adopted by secret ballot by 249 votes in favour and 15 against, with 165 abstentions—expresses the Conference's concern at the establishment of Israeli settlements in Palestine and in other occupied Arab territories, the economic and social consequences of which seriously affect the rights and interests of the Arab labour force. It calls upon the Israeli authorities to put an end immediately to the establishment of such settlements and to dismantle the existing ones, appeals to all States not to provide Israel with any assistance to be used specifically in connection with such settlements and requests the Governing Body of the ILO to provide various types of assistance to Arab citizens in these territories. The Director-General is requested to submit annual reports to the Conference on this subject.

The second resolution was adopted unanimously. Welcoming the accession to independence of Zimbabwe and the assistance already provided by the ILO, it requests the setting up of a new programme of assistance to that country with special emphasis on problems of re-settlement and vocational rehabilitation, vocational training, workers' education and leadership training.

The third resolution, which was also adopted unanimously, invites the ILO to promote and support rural development programmes (including agrarian reform) that aim at the eradication of poverty and at ensuring full employment and adequate nutrition and education, under conditions of freedom of association and equal treatment. It stresses the need for tripartite participation in all the activities contemplated.

Report of the Director-General

In his introduction to this year's report the Director-General looked back with some satisfaction on the results achieved by the ILO in 1979 in what had been exceptionally difficult circumstances. This was the second consecutive year in which the ILO had been working under severe budgetary constraints and yet, thanks largely to the full support of its tripartite membership, it had been a year marked by intense activity and substantial achievements.

1979 had seen a marked increase in technical co-operation activities: the ILO had been fortunate to obtain financial assistance from many quarters, including the UNDP and multi-bilateral aid donors, enabling it to expand its budget for technical co-operation by 26.7 per cent over that for 1978. This had made it possible to finance activities under the regular budget in fields such as workers' education and assistance to employers' organisations that attracted little extra-budgetary support.

At its 65th Session the International Labour Conference had renewed its commitment to the World Employment Programme by adopting, after a full-scale discussion, a resolution which had reiterated the urgency of implementing the Declaration of Principles and Programme of Action approved by the World Employment Conference in 1976.

The ILO had also made a substantial input to the FAO World Conference on Agrarian Reform and Rural Development, whose outcome had reflected an approach to the problems of rural development that had much in common with that of the ILO. The ILO's rural development activities had been examined by the Ninth Session of the Advisory Committee on Rural Development, which had reaffirmed the importance of anti-poverty programmes.

Neither had the ILO ignored the important social theme that was highlighted by the designation of 1979 as the International Year of the Child. Concentrating on areas where it could make a unique contribution, the ILO had published *Children at work*, which studied the problem of child labour and explored possible remedies, and had also participated in various national and international events organised within the framework of the IYC.

In 1979 a determined effort had been made to intensify ILO activities in the struggle against apartheid. In addition to convening a tripartite meeting to study labour questions in South Africa and various measures that might be adopted to combat apartheid, to which reference has been made above, assistance to national liberation movements in the countries neighbouring the Republic of South Africa had continued. A UNDP/ILO vocational training programme had enabled members of these movements to train at Turin and in institutes based in Africa. The Office had also begun to implement projects in Zimbabwe and Namibia designed to end discriminatory practices in labour matters.

Considerable progress had been made in one of the ILO's earliest and best known fields of activity, standard-setting. The International Labour Conference had adopted four new instruments and had begun discussions on an item concerning older workers. A high proportion of ratifications registered during the year under review had continued to come from developing countries. At its February-March 1979 Session the Governing Body had completed its in-depth review and classification of international labour standards, which would provide important guidelines for member States as well as enabling the Office to take stock of changing needs and views.

This year the Director-General devoted a special section of his report to training, "the challenge of the 1980s"—which he anticipated would be a decade of modest economic growth, fewer employment opportunities, rapid technological change and a sharp increase in world population. In particular, nearly 60 million young people would be added to the world labour force each year.

Could training help to solve the employment problem this tremendous influx implied? Bearing in mind that "people are the wealth of nations", it was important that training, while meeting the needs of the economy, should above all respond to the aptitudes and aspirations of the individual. Provided it did so, it would not only lead to improved employment opportunities but also open the door to career development and personal satisfaction as well as promote self-reliance and self-respect.

The task ahead was difficult and therefore it was necessary to concentrate on three major issues.

The first was equality of training opportunities. Too many social and economic barriers still denied certain groups a fair chance of receiving appropriate training—women, out-of-school youth, the disabled, migrant workers, rural dwellers, etc. Other obstacles, such as inherited values, high entry requirements, language problems and the lack of facilities, had also to be removed.

The second priority was to expand training opportunites, inter alia by encouraging undertakings to assume their responsibilities for training, providing more mobile training units and making greater use of the mass media.

Thirdly, it was necessary to improve the effectiveness and efficiency of training by securing more accurate information on employment market trends and establishing vocational guidance and counselling systems. Instructors also had to be trained and policies and programmes at the national, regional and sectoral level developed with the participation of employers' and workers' organisations.

This year, as a supplement to his report, the Director-General introduced the Medium-Term Plan for 1982-87. The Plan was neither a budget nor a blue-print for action but an attempt, based on an analysis of long-term labour trends, to help member States articulate their priorities for the 1980s in the field of ILO competence. The Plan addressed itself to two major tasks: the fight against poverty and injustice in the developing countries through concerted action to raise levels of employment, skills and conditions of work and life; and the pursuit of social progress in the more developed countries while promoting their adjustment to the new world economic order, both aims being pursued with full regard to the protection of human rights. Its discussion by the ILO's full membership represented at the Conference would give the Office valuable guidance in planning the ILO's programme and budget.

While putting the finishing touches to this year's report, the Director-General had learnt of the decision of the United States to resume membership of the ILO. The absence of the US, he said, had weakened the universality of the Organisation and deprived it of a wealth of experience in labour matters. Thus it was with particular satisfaction that he welcomed the US back as an invaluable ally in facing the challenges of the coming decade.

Discussion of the report

In the course of the debate that followed many speakers congratulated the Director-General on his initiative in introducing the Medium-Term Plan, which provided an opportunity for an exchange of views and encouraged member States to reflect critically on the challenges of the 1980s and what the ILO could do to meet them.

The majority of delegates also welcomed the section of the Director-General's report devoted to training and thought that he had chosen the right theme at a crucial moment. Emphasising the key role of training in the social and economic development of their own countries, they noted that it was particularly important at a time of recession or slow economic growth since it provided people with an opportunity to upgrade and update their skills or to enter a new occupation.

Many speakers stressed the need to intensify training activities in rural areas and extend them to the urban informal sector. Much more emphasis should be given, they urged, to low-cost, high-quality programmes which related directly to the needs of the poor in those areas. Special attention should also be devoted to other disadvantaged groups, especially women, migrant workers, the disabled and unemployed youth.

It was observed that the effectiveness of a national training system rested on two premises. The first was an educational system closely geared to the country's social and economic priorities and the second was the establishment of a fully fledged vocational guidance and counselling system. Training curricula and methodology had to be adapted to the cultural environment of the trainees, and it was also important that training activities should be co-ordinated by national bodies in which employers and workers were represented in order to ensure that programmes were relevant and wastage was minimised.

As for the International Centre for Advanced Technical and Vocational Training in Turin, the majority of speakers from developing countries thought that the Centre was of vital importance and that its future should be assured. Finally, stress was laid on the leading role played by the ILO within the UN system, where it was the organisation most directly concerned with the development of human resources through training.

The question of North-South co-operation and its links with, and effect on, the world employment situation was a recurrent theme in the debate. The deterioration of the employment situation in the North was prompting a move towards protectionist measures, and speaker after speaker emphasised the need to reverse this trend. A more dynamic growth process in the developing countries, it was argued, would greatly improve the prospects of growth in the industrialised countries through its effect on demand and employment. Thus trade liberalisation was necessary in order to reap the full benefits of the growing interdependence between North and South. In fact repeated reference was made to the recent symposium on this subject held in the ILO, which had shown that protectionism was a prescription for economic stagnation in both the North and the South.

The ILO's technical co-operation programmes were also in the forefront of the discussions. Most participants expressed their appreciation for the positive contribution made by the ILO to the elaboration and implementation of their countries' development programmes, and looked forward to further assistance.

The question of international labour standards was also fully debated. Speakers stressed the importance of laying down standards to govern job security, acceptable conditions of work, and employment creation. However, many representatives from the developing world felt that most ILO standards could be made more relevant to the social and economic circumstances prevailing in their countries. Delegates welcomed action already taken by the ILO to protect migrant workers and to improve their social benefits, especially through its Conventions and Recommendations, but the Office was called on to intensify its efforts to persuade host countries to eliminate the discrimination in labour matters that large numbers of migrants still suffered.

Many speakers shared the Director-General's view that the vast sums spent on armaments could be used instead to improve working and living conditions. They called on the ILO to do what it could to promote disarmament and to give special priority to studying its social and economic implications.

Sharing the general concern about the situation in the Middle East, many delegates urged the ILO to redouble its efforts to protect the rights and interests of the Arab workers in the occupied territories.

The Director-General's reply

After paying tribute to the quality of the discussions on his report, the report of the Governing Body and the Medium-Term Plan, the Director-General commented on the critical issues which had dominated the Conference. Impressed by the extent to which the participants had addressed themselves to the question of North-South relations, Mr. Blanchard clarified the ILO's position on this vital topic. Underlining the necessity of creating more "development-mindedness" among all nations, he warned against the dangers of the protectionist policies that were currently enjoying popularity in some industrialised countries and were creating a sense of injustice and resentment in a world that was more interdependent than ever before. In this connection Mr. Blanchard referred to the speeches of the two distinguished visitors who had addressed the Conference. President Caramanlis had stressed the need to attack the existing imbalance in North-South relations, failing which peace and prosperity would remain in jeopardy. Mr. Brandt had drawn attention to the need for the industrialised countries to encourage growth in the South by eschewing protectionism and facilitating adjustment to a new order of economic relations.

The Director-General assured delegates that the ILO was committed to helping both the North and the South to cope with the problems of the energy crisis, recession and adjustment to the changing world economic situation. The ILO would make its contribution by providing assistance in the fields of employment, training and technical co-operation. It had already hosted a symposium on the North-South dialogue and participated in the work that had led to the thoughtful and absorbing report of the Brandt Commission. As delegates had pointed out, the cost and availability of energy affected both the industrialised and the developing countries, and the ILO would accordingly study the effects of the energy problem on employment. In this connection greater use might be made of industrial committee and similar meetings which could deal, on a tripartite basis, with the problems of sectors especially affected by the repercussions of international competition and technological change.

As for the forthcoming Special Session of the UN General Assembly, which was to adopt the new development strategy for the 1980s and prepare the way for a new round of global negotiations, Mr. Blanchard told the Conference that the ILO had taken a very active part in seeking to ensure that the social aspects of development were given due priority in the new strategy.

Reminding delegates that, within the UN system, the ILO had a unique responsibility where training was concerned, Mr. Blanchard noted the prime interest of training to industrialised and developing countries alike. The task was immense, and priority had to be given to the poorest countries. Facilities should no longer be available only in large towns and cities but in rural areas too. The three regional training centres—ARSDEP, CIADFOR and CINTERFOR—would help workers' and employers' organisations to plan and operate their own training programmes. As for the Turin Centre, the Director-General reported that it was now operating at full capacity, and he stressed that it was complementary to, not in competition with, the three regional centres and national training institutions.

Recalling the assistance provided to Zimbabwe even before it became a Member of the ILO, Mr. Blanchard referred to the ILO's long-standing commitment to the elimination of apartheid and all other discriminatory practices, and expressed his satisfaction at the full debate that had been held on apartheid at this session.

Technical committees, where the essential work of the Conference was done, had this year achieved substantial results. Equality was one of the Organisation's cherished goals and the Director-General was pleased to see the Conference concerning itself with the question of equal treatment for men and women workers with family responsibilities. He also welcomed the adoption of the Recommendation concerning older workers. The Committee on Safety and Health had revised the list of occupational diseases, so vital to the improvement of working conditions, and had laid the groundwork for two new instruments concerning the prevention of occupational hazards.

Mr. Blanchard was pleased that delegates shared his opinion that the work of the Committee on the Application of Conventions and Recommendations was crucial to the Conference. Referring to the controversy generated—in bodies other than the ILO—over the question of minimum standards, he said he appreciated the importance attached to the observance of fair labour standards but he also understood the fears of certain countries that these might be little more than a form of disguised protectionism. The Office would undertake an objective study of the facts and bring the results before the Governing Body and the Conference.

On the question of freedom of association and labour relations the Director-General informed the Conference that, in November, he intended to submit to the Governing Body proposals in connection with a resolution adopted by the European Regional Conference in which he had been requested to undertake studies in certain European countries. Since the ILO had equal responsibilities to all member States, he intimated that similar studies might later be undertaken in other regions as well.

The Director-General drew attention to the Organisation's continuing budgetary constraints. The financial situation would remain precarious until the end of the 1980-81 biennium since the contribution of the United States would be used—as already reported—to cover the previous year's deficit and to reduce the contribution of member States in 1981.

Mr. Blanchard extended a warm welcome to all the new Members—Zimbabwe, Grenada, Viet Nam, Lesotho and St. Lucia—and to the United

States on its return to the ILO. He hoped that it would now be possible for the Organisation, strengthened as it was by its new Members, "to pursue objectives that are both ambitious and realistic, in response to the needs arising at the end of this millennium".

Notes

[1] The Recommendation, resolutions and other texts adopted by the Conference are reproduced in *Official Bulletin* (Geneva, ILO), 1980, Series A, No. 2.

[2] See *International Labour Review*, Nov.-Dec. 1979, pp. 665-668.

[3] ILO: *Older workers: work and retirement*, Reports IV (1) and (2), International Labour Conference, 66th Session, 1980.

[4] Idem: *Promotion of collective bargaining*, Reports V (1) and (2), International Labour Conference, 66th Session, 1980.

[5] The Committee had before it two reports prepared by the Office: *Equal opportunities and equal treatment for men and women workers: workers with family responsibilities*, Reports VI (1) and (2), International Labour Conference, 66th Session, 1980.

[6] See *International Labour Review*, Oct. 1975, pp. 240-243.

[7] ILO: *Safety and health and the working environment*, Reports VII *(a)* (1) and (2), International Labour Conference, 66th Session, 1980.

[8] The report of the meeting of experts is reproduced in idem: *Amendment of the list of occupational diseases appended to the Employment Injury Benefits Convention, 1964 (No. 121)*, Report VII *(b)*, International Labour Conference, 66th Session, 1980.

[9] The occupational diseases that have now been added to the list are as follows: diseases caused by the toxic halogen derivatives of aromatic hydrocarbons; infectious or parasitic diseases contracted in an occupation where there is a particular risk of contamination; hearing impairment caused by noise; diseases caused by vibration (disorders of muscles, tendons, bones, joints, peripheral blood vessels or peripheral nerves); diseases caused by work in compressed air; skin diseases caused by physical, chemical or biological agents not included under other items; lung cancer or mesotheliomas caused by asbestos; bronchopulmonary diseases caused by cotton dust (byssinosis), or flax, hemp or sisal dust; occupational asthma caused by sensitising agents or irritants both recognised in this regard and inherent in the work process; diseases caused by cadmium or its toxic compounds; diseases caused by fluorine or its toxic compounds; bronchopulmonary diseases caused by hard-metal dust; diseases caused by nitroglycerin or other nitric acid esters; diseases caused by asphyxiants: carbon monoxide, hydrogen cyanide or its toxic derivatives, hydrogen sulfide; diseases caused by alcohols, glycols or ketones; and extrinsic allergic alveolitis and its sequelae caused by the inhalation of organic dusts, as prescribed by national legislation.

International Labour Review, Vol. 119, No. 6, November-December 1980

New office technology and employment

David COCKROFT*

In the growing international debate on technology and employment it is being suggested that traditional relationships between investment, technical progress and employment no longer hold true: that certain recently discovered forms of technology will produce increases in industrial and service productivity so great and so widespread that output will not be able to expand fast enough to compensate, employment will fall, and in the absence of effective counter-measures unemployment will rise to unprecedented levels. Such views are not in fact new, but nor are they universally accepted. The United Kingdom Government's Central Policy Review Staff commented in late 1978: "The predictions made about employment that are now being made about microelectronics, were being made 20 or so years ago about earlier generations of computers. The UK Civil Service has used computers for a number of years and a study of the employment effects shows how wrong those predictions were".[1]

Despite the dangers inherent in long-term predictions, this article will try to show that there are potential problems associated with technological change which demand both serious analytical treatment and the development of sophisticated industrial and social policies.

1. The office sector

More people are employed in offices in the industrialised countries than in any other type of work. Even in the poorest countries office employment, particularly in areas such as banking, attracts the greater part of the highly qualified workforce. And in most economies the tertiary sector (which is to a large extent composed of office workers or workers in closely related occupations) is also the fastest growing source of employment, while the substantial proportion of office workers in manufacturing (and even in agriculture) should not be overlooked.

Since office jobs are concerned with processing information, they are particularly suitable for applying microelectronic-based "information

* International Federation of Commercial, Clerical, Professional and Technical Employees (FIET).

technology". One major problem in analysing this type of work is to identify and evaluate the office's output. Office productivity is conventionally measurable only in terms of the volume of paper produced, and while this can sometimes tell us how productive an individual worker is, the contribution of information technology can only be properly evaluated through its impact on the effectiveness with which the office as a whole performs the tasks allocated to it.

Most offices have two main types of worker. On the one hand, there are the "creative" workers who generate or analyse information using their own experience and judgement. On the other, there is the much larger group of workers who process information in a form acceptable to the decision-makers or who communicate it to workers in other offices or to the consumer. In most offices the majority of decisions are based largely on sets of instructions, or codes, and the clerks, executives or managers taking such decisions are "programmed" to carry out their tasks. Any task which can be logically defined in this way can in theory be automated. The much quoted but unfortunately unpublished "Office 1990" report by Siemens estimates that 40 per cent of all clerical-type jobs in the Federal Republic of Germany could be standardised and that 25-30 per cent could then be fully automated. In the public sector the estimate was much higher: 75 per cent of jobs could be standardised and 38 per cent automated.

The potential for reorganising office work to make it more efficient is thus very great, but in practice it is seldom fully realised. This will certainly change when the necessary equipment is cheap and plentiful enough to permit large-scale application. There are reasons to believe that this is now the case.

2. New office technology

In one sense there is very little "new" technology available today. The principles behind the equipment now being used to boost office productivity have been in existence for some time. The difference between what is available now and what was available five years ago is its flexibility, reliability, speed of operation, size and, above all, cost. The changes have been due chiefly to the phenomenal growth in the use of silicon integrated circuits and in particular of microprocessors and semiconductor memories. The most significant feature of microelectronic circuits is their very low marginal cost. Technological progress has roughly doubled the number of functions on a chip and halved the price per function every year. Because of the cheapness of the microelectronics, a "chip" with massive potential can still be used economically to do quite simple jobs.

Microprocessors have an enormous range of applications in the control and monitoring of manufacturing and other operations. Nevertheless, in the office they have the advantage of dealing directly with the commodity they are designed to process—information. Sophisticated transducers to turn mechanical movement into electronic information and vice versa are therefore not necessary. Office equipment currently available in Western markets includes word (or text) processors; small business computers; optical character recognition equipment; computer-controlled telephone exchanges and switching systems; facsimile transmitters; and mass electronic storage devices.

The technology itself is converging. Ten years ago there was little technical connection between the manufacture of typewriters (now developing into word processors), telecommunications equipment (then entirely electromechanical) and computers. Today the same skills, the same components and the same principles cover all three areas. The real importance of office technology is in the use of integrated office systems in which every product fits in with and encourages investment in the others.

Word processors

A word processor is an intelligent typewriter based on microelectronic technology and offering a large number of different facilities to increase the productivity of typing operations. A typical word processor consists of a keyboard, a visual display unit, a printer and some form of storage medium (usually magnetic discs), together with a central processing unit which gives the system "intelligence".

The practical consequences of word processing technology are extremely impressive. Productivity, measured in crude terms of letters or documents produced per man-hour, has been observed to increase by anything between 100 and 300 per cent.[2] Where large numbers of similar letters or successive drafts of documents have to be typed, word processing can make a huge difference to the speed and accuracy of the work done.

The most powerful influence on the use of word processing is likely to be price. The authors of a study for the UK Department of Employment found that in the course of preparing their report (less than 12 months) the cost per terminal of a word processing system had virtually halved. Estimates based on future prices of these systems envisage the total world market increasing from $944 million in 1977 to over $2,500 million in 1982.[3] Another source[4] suggests an annual growth rate in sales of 40 per cent.

Word processors will directly affect the jobs of typists, secretaries and some clerical workers—a significant but limited proportion of office workers. Of wider importance will be the increased use of data processing in the office through the introduction of small business computers.

Small business computers

World sales of small computer systems are estimated to have increased from $2,600 million in 1977 to $4,800 million in 1979—an annual growth rate of over 35 per cent.[3] This sales expansion has been achieved by large and continuing price reductions, greatly enhanced computing power, and the availability of standardised computer programmes. In physical terms small business computers are indistinguishable from screen-based word processors. It is the programmes which control the operation of the computer that are different.

Unlike traditional "mainframe" computers, small business systems do not require special air-conditioned rooms, they can fit into a standard office (often on a desk top), plug into a standard electricity supply, need relatively little and relatively unskilled labour to operate them, and can be used to standardise and automate any of a huge range of routine clerical and administrative jobs. However, it is the development of communications which turns a number of isolated technological developments into a truly integrated and universal information technology.

Office communications

The most common communications media in offices today are the telephone, the telex and of course the postal service. Some large organisations, chiefly US multinational companies, have an internal telecommunications switching network but most use the public telephone system. The high efficiency of communication between microelectronic devices results from the enormous speed with which digital information can be coded, sent along telephone wires and decoded. In the latter half of the 1980s many Western countries will move from electromechanical to digital telephone systems making high-speed data communications an even better economic proposition. The most common "new" communications device presently being used is the computer-controlled private telephone exchange: world sales in 1979 for this type of equipment are estimated at $1,160 million. Efforts are also being made to boost the efficiency of telex services by generating telex messages directly, e.g. from a word processor. The major elements in office communications will be high-speed text and data transmission and facsimile transmission—the speed of the latter is now being rapidly improved, which is crucial to the transmission of symbols, drawings, photographs and writing in scripts such as Chinese and Japanese that do not easily lend themselves to keyboard transcription.

The paperless office

Combined with the general availability of cheap powerful computers and advanced communications systems, the potential for storing information in electronic form is also increasing rapidly. Mass storage for computers is currently carried out by magnetic media which are either very expensive (discs) or very slow (tapes). A number of technological developments suggest that the problem of cheap and efficient electronic mass storage is on the point of being solved. Once this is done, the truly electronic office becomes economically feasible.

Less us look briefly at how such an office would work. Information would come in either from other electronic offices or in conventional form (by telephone or on paper). In the former case the information would be routed to the person responsible and held "on file" in a computer memory awaiting his/her attention. Information arriving in conventional form would be transcribed through a word processor (in the case of telephone conversations) or an optical character reader (in the case of printing on paper) into electronic form and fed into the system. The computer controlling incoming mail would also arrange to file the information centrally for future use. The information receiver (clerk, administrator, etc.) would be informed of the type and importance of incoming information on a visual display screen.

According to predetermined instructions, standard work would then be processed automatically by one or more computers, which would be able to consult both internal and external sources of information in order to do their job. Non-standard problems requiring the exercise of individual judgement would be referred automatically to the appropriate employee with an indication of its priority and "menu" of alternative decisions to choose from. The computer would prepare the appropriate forms, letters, documents, etc., to implement the decision made.

The flow of minor decisions to be made by the "creative" office worker would be drastically reduced. Access to information, whether internal or external, could be almost instantaneous, and available simultaneously to any number of users. The output of information would be either transmitted directly through the public or private telecommunications network to similar systems elsewhere or converted into paper-based sources for transmission by conventional means. The ratio of "servicing" to "creative" workers would be drastically reduced, and the functional efficiency of the office would increase beyond all recognition.

* * *

The above very brief technical description has covered only the technology applicable to general office work. Important developments are also taking place in the area of finance (automated tellers), in the retail sector (computer-controlled cash desk technology) and in the drawing office (computer-aided design).

One of the greatest difficulties in discussing the impact of technology on employment is knowing what the speed and pattern of assimilation of current technology into offices will be. Factors inhibiting the spread of new technology into office work include the conservatism of many decision-makers, the lengths to which some manufacturers of existing office equipment will go in order to maintain demand for their products,[5] and the comparatively high investment in existing capital stock, particularly in paper filing systems.

Finally, it may just not be physically possible for manufacturers both of chips and of office equipment to satisfy the demand. At present the growth of chip supply is exponential: more chips are produced each year than have ever been made before.[6] But it is generally expected in the semiconductor industry that this will begin to tail off. The estimated annual growth rate in dollar terms of the world semiconductor market is around 12 per cent, which is high compared with other markets but not astronomical. Even if the circuit elements available for commercial application grow by four times the dollar value, the current base is so small and the potential market so huge that it will probably be 15 years or more before the electronic office becomes the rule rather than the exception.

3. Office technology and employment

Many commentators on the new technology have suggested that it is likely to produce large-scale unemployment. Others (particularly governments) have argued that the dynamic process of cheapening products and expanding demand will continue as in the past to create new jobs to compensate for those rendered obsolete.

Productivity and output

It is of course a mathematical certainty that, in any national economy, if productivity grows faster than output the total number of man-hours employed will fall. Unless hours of work are reduced or more people work part time, total employment will also fall as a result. Productivity at the national level is generally measured by taking the over-all product of the economy and dividing by the number of man-hours employed. It is affected, inter alia, by changes in the sectoral balance of the economy (e.g. between manufacturing and services), by the behaviour of participants in the labour market (job protection measures) and by the effects of government social policies and the economic environment. Since in most national accounting systems the value of non-marketable services is not included in national output, increased employment in areas such as public administration automatically depresses productivity. This is true irrespective of the efficiency with which the people concerned carry out their jobs.

The late 1970s—the beginning of the microelectronics revolution—saw the slowest growth in productivity in the industrialised countries since the Second World War. The USA, the major source of advanced labour-saving and productivity-boosting equipment, actually had an absolute *fall* in productivity by 0.1 per cent per year between 1973 and 1980.[7] This was a result of the widespread recession which cut output by far more than it was possible or desirable to cut labour. It is clear therefore that even massive productivity increases in individual enterprises do not automatically have the same effect at the national level. Likewise, productivity improvements in one part of an organisation do not automatically raise that organisation's over-all productivity by the same amount. Most bureaucracies employ a significant number of people whose presence is more easily explained by the history of the organisation or the social needs of senior management than by their indispensable contribution to its work. These examples merely serve to emphasise that "productivity" is not a fixed, technologically determined parameter but a highly complex social, economic and technical variable. Technology exerts an important influence on national productivity, but by no means an overwhelming one.

Any calculation of labour displacement derived from productivity assumptions must also make an assumption about output. The normal approach of "pessimistic" forecasters is to take current macroeconomic projections of *low* output growth and superimpose on them high productivity growth rates due to new technology, thereby producing predictions of huge rises in unemployment. In the long term at least this is totally fallacious. Historically, periods of fast productivity growth have coincided with fast growth in output and relatively high levels of employment.[8]

In the long term productivity growth cannot and does not create unemployment. The problem is one of adjustment in the short and medium term, but this is not to minimise it. Even "transitional" or short-term employment is likely to create extreme bitterness amongst the workforce and seriously slow down further use of advanced technology. No one can estimate with accuracy how short the short term is in this context; besides, to suppose that a temporary period of adjustment will suffice takes no account of future developments in technology. What is needed is not ad hoc measures to cope with a particular type of new technology, but continuing political and institutional arrangements to ensure smooth adjustment to technological change in general.

Estimating the employment impact

It is unrealistic to suppose that accurate quantitative predictions can be made about the employment impact of new technology for individual national economies, let alone for the world as a whole. What may be possible and should be attempted, however, is to establish an internationally agreed methodology for estimating the impact in particular sectors and monitoring the employment situation for danger signals. In addition, a comprehensive data base of technological economic and social information is needed.

In the first place, research is needed on the capabilities of new technology both to replace people in existing jobs and to carry out tasks not currently done. For some types of equipment, e.g. word processors, there is no doubt about what they can do under controlled conditions. However, their performance *in situ* is a different matter. Most case studies on office technology look at a situation in which technological change has taken place and compare the conditions before and after. A well known example is the local government organisation in the UK where typing staff was reduced from 44 to 22 and the workload increased by an estimated 19 per cent through the use of word processing equipment.[4] But in this and similar cases little is known about external factors which may have affected employment levels, about the speed at which the change took place and the subsequent history of the workers whose jobs disappeared. Systematic studies using a standardised approach to cover a wide range of different sectors would help to overcome some of these problems. Case study work cannot, however, in itself answer questions about the over-all employment effects of technology. On the one hand, it ignores the positive effects of labour displacement on job creation in other enterprises or sectors. On the other, improved competitiveness may produce job losses elsewhere. As a US Government statistician recently remarked, "the employment impact of a technological change may occur long after the change has taken place and in an entirely different location".[9] The best that can be done through case studies is to estimate the range within which particular sorts of technology can affect employment.

Secondly, having established (however tentatively) what the technology can do, research is needed into how widely and quickly it is actually being applied. The most important factor bearing on the rate of assimilation is the balance of costs and benefits arising from office investment. For any machine that can displace labour by enabling fewer people to do the same volume and type of work, there is a break-even point where the cost of buying or renting the machine is roughly the same as the cost of employing the workers it can displace. For any standard typing job in the United States and other high labour cost countries, that point has already been passed by word-processing terminals, where a machine which improves productivity by 100 per cent can pay for itself in saved labour costs in less than six months. Similar break-even points are approaching or have been reached in electronic mail and filing and in data processing.

Even given the obvious cost-saving potential of the new technology, however, the nature of the pressure on employers will vary. In tight labour markets the trend towards new office technology will naturally be accelerated as employers seek to circumvent manpower shortages. However, there is growing evidence that enterprises faced with a stagnant economy and little likelihood of expanding output are also introducing new technology so as to reduce labour costs and improve profitability. Thus there is good reason to suppose that investment in information technology will continue at a high rate irrespective of the level of economic activity.

Information is also needed on the current and projected demand for and supply of various types of equipment on the world market. This information should be collected by impartial bodies and made freely available to all, not restricted to the small group of organisations which can afford to commission high-powered market research.

However much information is collected, though, the fundamental economic questions remain. If productivity expands significantly, then there must be either an expansion in total output at least as great as that expansion, or a reduction in the total number of man-hours worked. Tentative calculations made by FIET in 1978, for example, showed that an acceleration in the rate of growth of office productivity from 2½ per cent per year to 8 per cent would, combined with an unchanged rate of output growth, cut office employment in Western Europe by 5 million over a ten-year period. It is of course fallacious to suppose that output is autonomously determined without reference to productivity. But it is equally invalid to suggest that output automatically adjusts to provide full employment whatever the rate of productivity growth. If it did, there would not be over 20 million registered unemployed in the OECD area alone today and 300 million under- or unemployed in the developing countries. High growth rates and rising living standards in some sectors coexist with high unemployment and poverty in others, creating a dangerous and worsening world economic environment that threatens the process of technical change on which rises in living standards depend. The danger is particularly highlighted by the trends in the office and tertiary sector.

Traditionally, productivity growth has been much lower in tertiary sector occupations than in either manufacturing or agriculture. As a result, the tertiary sector has played a major role in job creation, particularly in the postwar period. In the EEC the share of services in total employment rose from 30 per cent in 1960 to 45 per cent in 1975. In the USA, between 1950 and 1978, while manufacturing output rose by 150 per cent for an employment growth of just over 30 per cent, the main service sectors grew by about 160 per cent for an employment growth of 150 per cent. Many of the new jobs created in the service sector, particularly at the lower levels of skill, have gone to women and to school leavers.[10]

The susceptibility of the tertiary sector to labour-saving technology threatens at the very least to curtail its traditional role as a source of expanding employment. The possibility also exists that employment in tertiary occupations could even drop. In structural terms this means fewer jobs for women and for the unskilled, particularly those straight from school. Since these groups are also the least well organised into trade unions they are much less likely to be able to resist such trends.

Turning briefly to the *qualitative effects* on office employment, it is possible to be somewhat more categorical. It is virtually certain that typing and shorthand will become less and less important in office work. Whether this results in a reduced over-all number of jobs is debatable, but there are a large number of office workers whose only skill is typing, and this could cause them severe personal readjustment problems. As for shorthand, within ten years in many offices the people currently dictating will be entering material themselves, probably using a simplified typewriter keyboard. If sophisticated voice recognition by computer becomes an economic proposition, the need for typists could disappear completely. Other office staff at some risk are filing clerks, messengers, telephonists and correspondence clerks. Generally it will be the less skilled jobs that are most affected, although some middle levels of management and administration which exist only to transmit information up and down could be eliminated by an effective internal communications system based on a computer. Middle-grade technical workers such as draughtsmen are also likely to be in much less demand as the use of computer-aided design—already widespread—extends even further. An analysis of qualitative job changes as a result of specified technical innovations is much easier to carry out by case study methods. The present paucity of material on the subject could usefully be remedied by the ILO and other well placed organisations.

Policy implications

It is difficult to escape the conclusion that there will be a serious unemployment problem in many countries over the next 10-15 years, and that advanced technology could significantly aggravate it. If this is to be avoided, the prime requirement is for public authorities to adopt economic and labour market measures enabling the various economies to adjust in a socially acceptable manner. These must include intelligent policies for manpower planning and the retraining of workers displaced from existing jobs as well as new forms of vocational training for future entrants to the labour market. Technology itself cannot be blamed for creating unemployment. It is the decision to employ it, the method of its implementation and the economic circumstances surrounding that decision which can reduce over-all employment opportunities. A policy of total opposition to job changes can only succeed in freezing an economy at its current stage of development and is a recipe for steady impoverishment. On the other hand, a policy of supine acceptance of any form of job loss as being for the common good is equally foolish if, as is too often the case, there is no adjustment mechanism providing workers displaced in one sector with suitable new jobs in another. There is a need to separate the concept of preserving *jobs* (i.e. the particular set of tasks carried out by a worker) from the more important concept of preserving *employment* (i.e. the availability of a job which he or she can do, is intrinsically satisfying and offers adequate wages and conditions).

4. The response of the trade union movement

The trade unions of the market economy countries are primarily concerned with preserving the jobs and living standards of their members against the threats posed by rapid changes in the world economic structure, consumer tastes and technology, and by the immense economic power of multinational companies. In the developing nations they are also concerned with seeing that their countries secure better terms for the transfer of technology and a fairer share of the world's industrial investment, production and income. One implication of new technology for the developing countries' trade unions is that they must consider the *quality* as well as the quantity of investment placed in their countries by multinational companies. It is certainly not true today, if it ever was, that investment automatically creates jobs. It can just as easily destroy them.

The initial response of the developed world's unions to the new question of microelectronic technology and employment has been extremely varied. Generally trade union policy statements or "reports" have tended to emphasise the job-destroying aspects of technology and have made proposals for modifying either technology policy or economic policy or both to alleviate what unions see as a severe unemployment problem growing in importance over the next two decades. They have tended to take a "pessimistic" attitude if only to balance the unrealistic optimism displayed by governments and employers.

In Europe formal statements of policy have been produced for example in the United Kingdom by the TUC as well as by a number of individual trade unions such as APEX,[4] the ASTMS[11] and the POEU.[12] In France a major report was prepared in 1977 by the CFDT,[13] while in Scandinavia, as well as individual publications by national centres, a special working group of the Nordic Council of Trade Unions has been established to monitor developments in technology. Trade unions in most other European countries (e.g. the Federal Republic of Germany, Italy, Belgium) have produced detailed research and educational material analysing the impact of technology on their own national economies or providing policy guidelines for their negotiating officers. At the European level the European Trade Union Institute in Brussels has published a major analytical report on the subject.[14]

Outside Europe, interest in questions of technology has been greatest in Australia and New Zealand. Virtually every trade union in both countries has produced detailed research and policy material on the subject, and pressure from the unions in Australia, particularly in the telecommunications sector, led to the Government setting up a Commission of Enquiry (the Myers Commission) into technological change. In the United States, partly in response to the European trade unions' energetic approach, American unions have begun to give serious thought to the question. A conference was organised in June 1979 by the AFL-CIO

Department for Professional Employees and the proceedings were recently published.[9]

Growing appreciation of the impossibility of dealing with technological questions in a piecemeal fashion has led unions to place more emphasis on international activity. In addition to the European level, international trade union secretariats—including my own (FIET),[15] the International Metalworkers' Federation (IMF)[16] and the Postal, Telegraph and Telephone International (PTTI)[17]—have produced studies and policy statements or held conferences of national union experts. Other international union bodies such as the ICFTU and the Trade Union Advisory Committee to the OECD have also shown increasing interest in the subject, and a resolution on new technology proposed by workers' delegates from ICFTU-affiliated organisations was adopted at the ILO's Third European Regional Conference in 1979.

The commonest points making up the "trade union view" are as follows:

— New forms of microelectronics technology on the factory floor and in the office are likely, unless influenced by deliberate policy, to cause a loss of jobs in the advanced countries in the foreseeable future. Opinions about the extent of the job loss, the time-scale and the sectors most affected differ. Governments should undertake objective studies and monitor developments.

— A policy of outright opposition to technological change is impracticable and/or undesirable. No country can maintain employment by keeping its technology unchanged while its competitors move on and reduce costs. In any event, the productivity increases made possible by new technology provide the means for improvements in workers' living standards.

— The main responsibility for avoiding large-scale unemployment lies with governments, which should pursue expansionist economic policies designed to stimulate growth, and active manpower policies to help the labour market adjust.

— The smaller number of man-hours' work available should be translated into shorter working time for more people. Some unions describe this as "work sharing", others object to the term. Reductions in the working week, longer holidays and earlier retirement are all legitimate objectives for trade unions.

— Governments should try to discourage labour-displacing uses of technology. Some unions, e.g. in Sweden, suggest a "technology tax" to alter the relative costs of capital and labour. Manufacturers of electronic equipment and systems as well as organisations using them should be made to take more account of social needs. Agreements on job security should be negotiated with employers.

— Industrial democracy and participation schemes should be extended to give workers an effective say over the application of new technology in the workplace. Some unions go further and suggest specific legislation giving the workers/unions an effective veto. The Australian Council of Trade Unions' proposal of a five-year moratorium on all job-displacing technology can be considered an extreme example of this approach.
— Workers should be protected against deterioration in the content or skill requirement of their jobs and against machinery which could dehumanise their work (e.g. by subjecting them to humiliating degrees of control) or adversely affect their health (e.g. the possible effects of visual display units on eyesight).
— Trade union representatives should be given training both by their union and by their employer in the basic principles of computer and telecommunications technology. Systems design should be made a participative process with union representatives and management jointly setting the parameters round which the technologists elaborate the system.

5. Conclusions

The types of technology discussed in this article could have serious employment consequences in the industrialised world which, if they occur, will feed through to lower employment levels and lower living standards in the developing countries. Even if, on some economists' time-scale, the job loss generated causes only "transitional" unemployment, the expectations of workers, the sophistication of communications and the strength of organised labour will combine to react against a mechanism which puts the burden of adjustment on the backs of working people. In assessing whether it is politically and economically possible to avoid the negative aspects, the period over which change is expected is crucial. If the electronic office becomes a reality in five years' time, nothing can be done. If, as is more likely, it takes 15 or 20 years, all that is required is to start the adjustment process now.

There is wide agreement that opposition to technology *per se* is not a viable policy response. Yet opposition is encouraged by the attitude of electronics multinationals, supported by some governments, which offer workers the choice between "new technology" and "no technology". There is no such simple choice. The potential which microelectronics puts at our disposal in industry and in the office can be used in countless different ways. The decision to develop technology in particular directions is determined not by technical factors but by economic and social influences. If something will not sell, it will not be manufactured.

Even beyond the question of technical development, however, the employment effects of computer-based equipment depend on how the system itself is designed and implemented at the local level. There are an infinite number of ways in which a computer system can be introduced into a given office. Where technologists or managers present workers with a *fait accompli*, this reflects economic, social and political decisions which they have already made but have cloaked in the guise of "technology".

The objective for trade unions, governments and employers should be to implement technological change in a way which avoids large-scale unemployment, promotes high geographical and occupational mobility and distributes the fruits of increased productivity in an equitable way. Appropriate policies will have to be shaped at all levels.

Without doubt the first priority for governments is to abandon engineered recession as a means of controlling inflation and energy consumption and to enter into partnership with unions and employers to find the best means of stimulating non-inflationary growth. In particular, international agreements on a massive increase in development aid from the industrialised countries, as recommended in the Brandt Commission report, coupled with cuts in the enormous world-wide expenditure on armaments should greatly expand the demand for goods and services using productivity-boosting technology.

Second, governments should take a deliberate political decision to give high priority to employment creation. This will entail large public expenditure on such things as training in the new skills required; placement services; investment assistance for the creation of more jobs; and intensive research into the effects of different types of technology.

Third, governments should create a favourable climate for employment changes. This means giving a high degree of income support to workers displaced by new technology, encouraging full transferability of all pension and other accrued rights from job to job, and legislating in favour of earlier retirement as well as other initiatives to reduce total working time.

Fourth, industrial policy—including stimulation of the production and application of microelectronic components—should take account of social needs. The key multinational companies which control the research, development and marketing of high-technology products should be placed under firm international control.

Last, governments should encourage the extension of industrial democracy, consultation, negotiation and information rights of trade unions whose members are affected directly or indirectly by technological developments. This is not to imply that such consultation is only now justified because of new technology. However, the potentially vast changes arising from the use of microelectronics accentuate the need to transform industrial relations so that workers everywhere may participate in decisions affecting their own jobs.

Consultation with trade unions should be undertaken at the earliest possible stage—when the options for technology use are still open. The ease with which advanced technology is applicable in the office has already provided a major stimulus to white-collar unionisation. This trend will continue and employers must decide quickly whether to try to fight it or to react in a positive way: they should be brought more and more to the negotiating table both to explain the benefits and to justify the costs to their employees' representatives. Participative methods of systems design should be practised as a matter of routine.

For unions, employers and public authorities there must be a changed approach to employment planning. The emphasis must shift from defending jobs to expanding employment. It is an inevitable result of any technical change that the pattern of jobs done will alter. Unquestionably, microelectronics will have far-reaching effects on white-collar employment in industrialised countries. However, it is a matter of political choice whether these take place smoothly or disruptively, and whether the cost of a dynamic economy is borne mostly by older workers who cannot retrain, married women forced out of the labour market and young unskilled workers unable to find permanent employment. Provided economic, manpower and industrial relations policies become more directly attuned to the problem of creating enough new, better paid, higher skilled and more satisfying jobs to satisfy the demand, and provided the necessary changes in the attitude of employers and trade unions take place, the enormous potential benefits which microelectronic technology promises in the office, in the factory, in the home and in education can and will be realised.

Notes

[1] Central Policy Review Staff: *The social and employment implications of microelectronics* (London, 1978), p. 6.

[2] Even official studies (which are often concerned to minimise fears about technology) accept that word processors can have very significant effects. To quote a recent UK Department of Employment study, "a reasonable consensus has emerged ... that by using word processors over the generality of typing tasks—that is to say not employing them exclusively upon those typing tasks for which they are especially suited—productivity gains of something in excess of 100 per cent can be obtained". J. Sleigh, B. Boatwright, P. Irwin and R. Stanyon: *The manpower implications of micro-electronic technology* (London, HM Stationery Office, 1979), p. 61.

[3] *Chips in the 1980s*, Special report No. 67 (London, Economist Intelligence Unit, 1979).

[4] Association of Professional, Executive, Clerical and Computer Staff: *Office technology—the trade union response* (London, 1979).

[5] *Computer Weekly* (London), 31 Jan. 1980.

[6] *The Economist* (London), 23 Feb. 1980, p. 84.

[7] *OECD Economic Outlook* (Paris), Dec. 1979, p. 25.

[8] Trades Union Congress: *Employment and technology: report by the TUC General Council to the 1979 Congress* (London, 1979), p. 10.

[9] See AFL-CIO Department for Professional Employees: *Silicon, satellites and robots* (Washington, 1979).

[10] ILO: *Growth, structural change and manpower policy: the challenge of the 1980s*, Report of the Director-General, Third European Regional Conference, Geneva, 1979.

[11] Association of Scientific, Technical and Managerial Staffs: *Technological change and collective bargaining* (London, 1979).

[12] Post Office Engineering Union: *The modernisation of telecommunications* (London, 1979).

[13] Confédération française démocratique du travail: *Les dégâts du progrès—les travailleurs face au changement technique* (Paris, 1977).

[14] European Trade Union Institute: *The impact of microelectronics on employment in Western Europe in the 1980's* (Brussels, 1979).

[15] FIET: *FIET Conference on Computers and Work*, Velm, Austria, November 17-18, 1978 (Geneva, 1979); idem: *Computers and work: FIET action programme* (Geneva, 1979).

[16] International Metalworkers' Federation: *Effects of modern technology on workers* (Geneva, 1979).

[17] Postal, Telegraph and Telephone International: "Trade unions and new technology in postal and telecommunications services", statement adopted by the PTTI's 15th European Regional Conference, Stockholm, September 1979, in *PTTI Studies* (Geneva), No. 25, Winter 1979.

International Labour Review, Vol. 119, No. 6, November-December 1980

Speculations on the social effects of new microelectronics technology

A. B. CHERNS *

Microelectronics technology will affect us all. But it will affect us in different ways. It will expand the range and raise the quality of existing products. It will foster new products and processes. It will accelerate the communications revolution. As consumers, we will all experience some of these developments to a large degree and all of them to some degree. But as producers we will be differentially prone to dislocation of our working lives. Some will be displaced from jobs or industries which microelectronics will render obsolete. Others will be employed in the microelectronics industry or in the new industries that microelectronics will promote. The consequences for employment as a whole are nowhere known. Many claim that the loss of jobs will be of calamitous proportions; others argue that similar fears were expressed when computers were first introduced but the predicted disaster failed to occur. But it seems clear that some industries will be affected sooner and more gravely than others; that therefore some categories of workers, some regions and some countries will be hit especially hard.

Even before the impact of the new technology has been felt, we have been witnessing the so-called de-industrialisation of established industrial regions in the face of competition from the newly industrialised countries of the Third World. Over the last 25 years we have seen the trend towards "post-industrialism" in North America and Northern and Western Europe; fewer people employed in manufacturing, especially in the older and labour-intensive industries; more employed in service industries and the public sector; a growth of white-collar at the expense of blue-collar work. These trends have accompanied the movement of married women into paid employment. While the advanced industrial societies have moved towards post-industrialism, the newly industrialised countries have built industries that are beginning to displace the older manufacturing sectors of Europe and North America, and even of Japan.

* Head of Department and Professor of Social Sciences, Department of Social Sciences, University of Loughborough, England.

The remainder of the Third World struggles to create industrial employment and to ease the burden of imports, torn between the efficiency of high technology and the misery of high unemployment.

We must expect the new microelectronics technology to affect these different groups in different ways. When we turn to its probable effects we shall need to remember these distinctions.

Values in society: "post-materialism"

Without going into the question of what caused what, we know that the trend in the advanced industrial countries towards post-industrialism has been accompanied by a shift in values towards "post-materialism", a shift which now causes concern to those who see post-industrialism as a decline into dependency or poverty. The post-materialist values represent a complex of attitudes towards economic, political and social issues; while broadly liberal and permissive on social issues, they tend to be egalitarian and consumer-oriented on economic ones. Most prominent is an insistent humanitarianism and urge towards the exploration and fulfilment of self. Post-materialist attitudes towards work emphasise its role in obtaining self-fulfilment, rather than money or security or power. One study found that, even in the richest countries with the broadest base of tertiary education, the proportion of people professing post-materialist values is still under 15 per cent, with a quarter professing materialist and the remainder mixed values.[1] Their importance for the future is, however, underlined by the steady trend away from materialism as one descends the age scale; people aged 16-25 were found to be markedly more post-materialist; in the Federal Republic of Germany they were as numerous as the materialists and in Belgium outnumbered them.[2]

In a recent poll (November 1977) of the EEC countries, when offered a choice between more pay and shorter hours, over 50 per cent of the worker respondents in Belgium, Denmark, France, the Federal Republic of Germany, the Netherlands and the United Kingdom chose the latter (64 per cent in the Netherlands and 66 in Denmark).[3] The value shift is real and not simply associated with youth; it has been shown that cohorts as they age lose little of their post-materialism. The effect is real too. Commenting on the dearth of skilled men alongside high unemployment, *British Public Opinion*[4] commented that skilled men leaving the engineering industry often chose such occupations as bus driving and milk delivery. Undergraduates shun production and technical management, opting for broadcasting, journalism and public relations: "The key perhaps lies with the factors which are important to students in choosing their careers. There is strong emphasis on immediate job satisfaction. Long-term career opportunities and training which provides a marketable asset were less important, although ranking above a high starting salary."

The five most important factors were: (1) sufficient intellectual challenge; (2) full and constructive use of time; (3) responsibility; (4) opportunity to work with people rather than things; and (5) opportunity to be creative and original. Freedom from supervision ranked slightly above high starting salary. It is likely that the attraction for the skilled men of bus driving and milk delivery was their freedom from supervision. And it should be emphasised that Britain had, along with Denmark, the smallest proportion of youthful post-materialists in any of the 11 countries studied in 1972-73.[5]

Since one of the factors enabling the newly industrialised countries to make rapid industrial progress has been the apparent willingness of their workforces to accept the traditional industrial disciplines, forecasts of the impact of microelectronics need to take account of the different value bases of different parts of the world.

The potentialities of the microprocessor: options for getting society's work done

The potentialities of the microprocessor are widely discussed and widely speculated upon. All agree that it permits the capability of a large computer to be concentrated into a small space at low cost in both money and energy. I do not need to rehearse here all the marvels of microtechnology. What I want to emphasise are two aspects of its capabilities.

On the one hand microelectronics brings the robot factory within sight. The automation which the computer foreshadowed is brought infinitely nearer by the "smartening" of devices now able to carry out their own sensing functions, by the keyboard access it provides to the numerically controlled machine, and by the instant presentation of complete process information.

On the other hand, by making possible the provision of information "on line" which would formerly have required the real time of a large computer and by enabling its rapid direct communication, the microprocessor removes much of the penalty of distance.

It is of course easier to imagine how the microprocessor will enable us to do what we already do more quickly, more cheaply and more accurately; it is less easy to imagine different ways of doing what we do now, and less easy still to imagine our doing totally different things. And what we shall want to do is a product not only of our ingenuity, but also of our values and needs. The same facilities can be put to use in a thousand different ways, for fun or for real. Indeed, among the earliest things that people thought of doing with the computer was to programme it to play chess; among the early uses of the microprocessor was the devising of television games. I would argue that it is difficult to imagine a society in which that did not occur, one that was ingenious enough but not so playful.

Play and originality are inseparable, not only because our earliest flights of imagination are in play, important though that is, but also because the relaxation of control over conscious thought that is needed for creative work is the relaxation of play. That should lead us to expect that many of the serious things that microprocessors will be doing in the future will be first encountered in unserious things. It is very tempting, as well as very easy, to adopt a censorious view of the trivial uses of invention when so much of a serious nature requires to be done. But that kind of criticism would inhibit the emergence of the truly original.

It seems probable that we may come to look differently upon the whole process of production and man's role in it. We have already changed our view of man and machine from that of the machine as aid, through man as operator of machine, to man as monitor of machine. When so much of the best of man's knowledge and performance can be programmed into the machine and unerringly reproduced on demand, the machine becomes the monitor of man.

To make use of the possibilities which the microprocessor opens for us, we need to reconsider what kind of society we want to have, what are the implications of different ways of looking at man and his machines. The use we make of the new technology should depend upon our choice of what constitutes a decent life, rather than the other way round as has unfortunately been the practice hitherto. It now seems likely that different societies will make different use of the microprocessor, which has as much capacity for divergence as for convergence: some societies will use the microprocessor to enhance humanist values, while others will use it to strengthen the domination of individuals by institutions, including work organisations and the State itself.

Centralisation or decentralisation?

The new technology removes the old limits to both centralisation and decentralisation at all levels of organisation. Because the microprocessor makes communication and the provision of information so easy, so quick and so cheap, it also makes it possible to centralise control. Centralised control has hitherto suffered from the difficulties of providing and processing all the necessary information and from the inefficiencies of communication of decisions and feedback. Consequently authority has to be delegated. But as it is delegated to people who do not have the whole picture, nor the responsibility for it, their actions are necessarily sub-optimal for the system as a whole. The microprocessor removes much of the difficulty of centralising information and of the inefficiencies of communication. Furthermore, so much can be programmed in advance that the overload of decision-making at the centre can be radically reduced.

Equally, decentralisation has suffered from the difficulties of providing information. Whereas with centralisation the problem is to know what is happening at the periphery, what special needs the periphery has or what difficulties it is encountering, with decentralisation the problem lies in providing the periphery with information about how decisions at local level affect the attainment of over-all goals and how they affect the functioning of other points on the periphery. Again the microprocessor offers us the possibility of providing at each point on the periphery a picture of the functioning of the system as a whole and of the actions of other peripheral points. Information is like butter; you can heap it all on one central plate or distribute it over the plates of every diner. The difference is that with a limited amount of butter you cannot do both; with information you can. In the decentralised pattern local decision-makers may need to communicate with one another; in the centralised pattern they all communicate with the centre.

Since the new technology has the capacity for both, it could very well be that societies or governments or organisations with a preference for centralisation will use it to strengthen their tendency to centralise, while those that prefer decentralisation will decentralise further. The questions, then, are: Which is likely to turn out to be the more efficient? What are the longer-term consequences of one or the other choice? What are the likely difficulties? It can be argued that the more uncertain the environment and the more it differs from point to point on the periphery, the greater the chances of survival of the decentralised over the centralised approach. It is also arguable that where centralised control depends upon denying information to the periphery, the microprocessor makes it more difficult as it becomes harder and less defensible to continue that denial. Even if both these arguments are valid they do not, in my view, lead to the certainty that there will be a convergence towards decentralisation; not all environments are so variable, not all values so opposed to control. What is more likely is that the two will coexist. We have already some evidence as to the conditions under which decentralisation occurs in work organisations.

Decentralisation and the quality of working life

Current quality of working life programmes all emphasise the decentralisation of control and decision-making, often to autonomous or semi-autonomous working groups. If we consider where the quality of working life approach has made most headway we note that *(a)* it has gone furthest in process industry, especially where high technology involves high capital investment per worker; *(b)* it has tended to be taken up in organisations with multiple plants rather than in firms with single locations; *(c)* the advance has been greatest in societies which have undergone rapid social change, where the generation gap has been widest; and *(d)* the impetus for new forms of organisation has come predominantly from the top or near the top.

Let us consider the meaning of these phenomena.

(a) High-technology process industry, because it involves high capital investment per worker, also depends very heavily on the workers' understanding of what is happening and on their motivation.[6] It is essential that they should intervene before the process goes out of control and they must therefore have, and be able to use, adequate information about how the process is going. In that situation you cannot afford to have all the knowledge and all the decision-making power locked up in supervisors who may be busy elsewhere or not available when action is urgently required. It is not that the environment of such work is exceptionally unstable or unpredictable; it is that the penalty for failing to act appropriately when the environment varies is unacceptable; what matters is the *product* of environmental uncertainty and the cost of failure to adapt to it.

(b) Organisations with multiple plants have already had to accept a considerable measure of decentralisation and have learned to live with it. They have also learned that this provides them with some room for experiment; they do not have all their eggs in one basket.

(c) Many organisations in countries where the young most strongly embrace the post-materialist values recognise that the old forms of work organisation may not attract enough workers in the future to survive. As we have seen, even in Britain, many prefer autonomy to the possibility of a career, if the latter involves subjection to the customary forms of work organisation. The experience of Volvo was salutary; top management recognised that it was becoming virtually impossible to recruit Swedes for work on the assembly line.[7]

(d) The impetus has come from high levels in the organisation mainly because it is only in an already highly decentralised one that it could effectively come from anywhere else. In a centralised organisation you have to convince the top, and the lower down you are the less your chance. Nor has the impetus come from outside, from the unions for example, though where associations of unions and employers have embraced the quality of working life notion, usually with the government as an active third party, the pressure has again come from above.

Effects on white-collar work

I mentioned above the conditions under which the new technology is most likely to be used to favour decentralisation and work group autonomy. My discussion was there confined to manufacturing technology. Yet we are all aware, and to some extent apprehensive, of the impact the new devices will have in the domain of white-collar work.

Because quality of working life considerations have entered this domain more recently, it is less easy to be precise about the new technology's effects. Banks, insurance companies, government offices and many other organisations have introduced the computer; most have used it in such a way as to fragment jobs and reduce the employee's autonomy. Hospitals using the computer for monitoring and control functions have encountered the resentment of nursing staff newly experiencing dependence on the machine. Computerised warehouses have reduced or eliminated the skills of storekeeping and the self-supervision of warehousemen. Word processing departments have centralised and devalued the secretary. Some organisations have now recognised the diseconomies that result from such applications and have attempted to redesign jobs accordingly. Invariably the redesign seeks to restore interest in the job by restoring the link of clerk with client or by assigning more responsibility and autonomy to clerks (or other white-collar workers), either individually or in groups.

Apart from this, it is harder to discern a pattern in the introduction of quality of working life issues into work redesigns in white-collar organisations than in manufacturing industries. The only generalisation I can offer is that the need for such redesigns has become most clear where computerisation has come early and has bitten deep. So far it is fair to say that redesign has done no more than restore in a few organisations the skills and autonomy that went with clerical jobs before the computer reduced them; I cannot report any instance of the computer being deliberately used to upgrade clerical jobs.

Freedom of choice and determinism

We may conclude that the ways in which the new technology is used will greatly depend upon factors such as those we have discussed, factors which reflect national patterns of industrial organisation, social structures and values and political arrangements. The microprocessor offers choice. Of course all technology is a matter of choice, a truism often obscured by its apparent determinism. Once the choice is made it appears inevitable; in the light of the technology we now possess, the choices that led to its emergence appear not to have been choices at all; a steady progression can be discerned, the blind alleys are forgotten.

Our attitudes towards technology are still deterministic; we perceive those who resist the introduction of new technology as hostile to change, defending old rights and old ways, modern Luddites. The resisters in their turn mount their attack against the technology rather than against the uses to which it will be put, or insist that the new technology be used to maintain established ways of working and living. Thus the full range of choice is seldom debated.

But it would equally be a mistake to conclude that technology is itself determined entirely by the nature of society. It is true that a closed society may be oblivious of, or unable to find any use for, a discovery or an invention. But most societies at most times are open and can be greatly influenced by innovations elsewhere or by chance occurrences at home.

And the public discussion of the microprocessor together with its undoubted potential for widespread and momentous changes increase the probability that choices will both be made and be seen to be made. In fact as public interest and concern with technology have been growing in recent decades, and new institutional instrumentalities for scrutinising and challenging it have been making their appearance and granted political influence by legislation in some countries, the course that microelectronics technology takes may be more clearly the outcome of deliberate choice, publicly made, than has ever been the case before. Hitherto the choice of how to introduce the computer, what work to assign it, has been less free than its potentialities warranted. Firms selling computers have of course been anxious to demonstrate their wonders to the full. Very early on they learned that they must design software to their customers' special requirements. They hired and trained systems analysts to determine what the customer's operations were, how they could be modelled and controlled. But all involved in the design process shared implicit views about the roles of man and machine, striving always towards the routinising of work. They shared, too, a belief in the necessity of hierarchy within organisations, and in their designs they reinforced it. To the engineer the perfect machine is the one that an imbecile could operate; he is surprised if the result is a machine only an imbecile is happy operating. Thus the choices were constrained by the assumptions about people, about jobs and about organisations that were brought in with the computer in the heads of the systems designers.

It is of course certain that as man is born to make mistakes, similar or even worse mistakes will be made with the microprocessor. But some of the characteristics of the microprocessor may make certain good choices more likely. As I have already indicated, the opportunities for decentralisation are greatly enhanced, though this does not mean they will be taken.

The future of work and employment

Whether the opportunities held out by the new technology are taken or not will depend on the nature of the societies which will develop with the aid of the microprocessor. Utopians have always had a vision of a society which does not rely on the unremitting toil of most of its members. But the Utopias of the Garden of Eden or of Heaven or of Arcadia are simple and unsatisfying to the modern taste. We are frightened of leisure and we find it hard to imagine life without work. Unsurprisingly, then, there is no model of a leisured society.

The new technology does not promise one tomorrow. But it is plain that in the industrialised countries the same amount of goods and services requires fewer man-hours to produce each year. These countries look to "growth" to maintain levels of employment. As growth has recently slowed or ceased, unemployment has risen and average working weeks have begun to decline. Productivity has continued to increase in almost all. (Writing in Britain I am careful to include the qualification "almost".) Before micro-electronics has even begun to make its inroads, the modernisation of older, comparatively labour-intensive industry has been displacing workers faster than new industry can absorb them. And as new industries are capital- rather than labour-intensive the struggle to maintain full employment becomes harder all the time.

Clinging as always to old models of society, governments and commentators express alarm, the former seeking frenziedly to "create" employment. The simple solution to the "problem of unemployment"—spreading work by reducing hours of work—is advanced by unions and rejected by employers, who perceive it as nothing but a subterfuge to hoist wages by increasing the hours paid at overtime premiums. All accept that unemployment is a problem. Part of that perception results from the analysis of unemployment as a waste of resources, as indeed it was when production was held below installed capacity by deficiency of demand. Unemployment is also seen as a social evil when it places its victims outside the ranks of full citizenship. Entwined with this is the view of work as an essential element in man's life, the notion that without work he is not a full man.

But are work and employment mere synonyms? Is to be out of work the same thing as to be unemployed? In our societies we fail to draw the distinction. And at the same time as we aim to put people who are out of work into employment, we seek to take the work out of employment. Because we have confused work with employment we would rather see people idle on a payroll than busy without pay. Why? Because we rely on employment to distribute resources. People are either "workers", that is employees, full citizens, or they are dependants of workers—children preparing for employment, or housewives, or pensioners retired from employment. To such an extent has employment become the requirement for full membership of society that housewives, deprived of the sense of full citizenship, do not know whether to demand the opportunity to seek employment outside their homes or to demand wages for working in them, thus becoming "employed". Worshipping the fetish of employment, we confer on the own-account worker the absurd description "self-employed". Why is it so great to be employed? Work may be ennobling, but is not employment demeaning?

As our society has industrialised, so has the entitlement of the citizen to a share in its resources shifted from the possession of a "status" and the performance of the obligations that accompanied it to the possession of employment. Obviously, a society which relies so heavily on employment as a means of distributing material and moral resources (respect, prestige, etc.) is gravely shaken by the impact of too little employment. The micro-processor is feared not because it will lead to the production of less wealth but because it will enable wealth to be produced with less employment. Of course that wealth has to be distributed, people have to acquire a right to demand a proportion of it, but why do they need to be "employed" for that purpose? At once the litany of objections is recited. "Somebody will have to work; if people can get what they want without working, who will want to work?" "Without everybody at work, how is the wealth to be created?" And so on. It is very hard indeed to think afresh about so fundamental an element of our social structure, to see society with so central a prop removed.

The antithesis of employment and idleness is a false one. Equally misleading is the confusion of price with value. A whole series of cherished beliefs will have to be sacrificed. Let us start our holocaust by putting to the sword the ideas that education is for the young, work for the young and middle-aged adult, and leisure for the old—ideas derived from the needs of an industrial civilisation.

I do not want to suggest that overnight we shall find that all necessary work can be done by microelectronic slaves, nor that we can dismantle the structures which distribute wealth and status and replace them easily. But if, as does appear credible, progressively more of the tasks performed by men can be taken over by machines so that the creation and distribution of goods and services will never again require 65,000 hours of everyone's life, we shall need to acquire the values that go with the sequestration of a mere 35,000 or 25,000 hours. They will not be the values of today any more than the values of today are those of the citizens of the Athenian republic.

Whether a period of employment will become a form of public service expected but not demanded from each citizen or whether it will become the lot of a new aristocracy or a new helotry depends upon the system of values which will emerge. If the transitions are gradual, the new values may sustain a continuity between present and future; if millions are unemployed for many of their early years, the dislocations of value systems would be sharp and lead to violence against existing institutions, with unpredictable consequences. The management of transition is the vital factor.

If work is a real physical, psychological and social need for man and employment comparatively scarce and not a human need, we shall have to revise our identification of work with employment and leisure with idleness. We shall also have to revise our measures of welfare. There is no need to rehearse once more the deficiencies of GNP per head as a measure of welfare. But its retention failing a better distorts our policies. If I decorate my house, I am using my leisure—no gain accrues to the GNP. If an organisation employs and pays me to do so, I am working and the GNP rises. If, through the benefits of technology, both methods became equally efficient in the utilisation of resources of time and energy, our present measures would favour the second, organisational solution. So long as there are real gains in efficiency measured on really appropriate criteria it may be in the interests of society as a whole that we prefer organisation and employment. But our present measures are so biased in their favour that we are liable to persist in that preference beyond the point at which it ceases to make sense and to miss noticing when we have reached the stage at which the preference should be reversed.

There will always remain large sectors of activity where the benefits of scale and division of labour are overwhelmingly great. But we have already organised beyond that point. Not only are diseconomies of scale experienced in manufacture, they have become clear in hospitals and schools; we have become aware of the disbenefits of organisation in our welfare services. I am not arguing that small is always beautiful; what I am saying is that the dice are loaded in favour of the large and the organised, that although in some respects that may have been an advantage in the past it will be dangerous if continued into the future.

Microelectronics will probably enable many things to be done on a smaller scale than now, some of which are already obvious, some less so. Among the obvious are the bringing of the power of the computer to the desk top, the functions of the telephone exchange to the office, or even the home. Among the less obvious are the possibilities for smaller, yet efficient, electricity generators uncoupled from the grids, which themselves consume a sizeable fraction of the power they transmit. Many, though not all, of the capabilities of microelectronics make decentralisation and smaller size more efficient. How will that fit in with the contraction of employment and the shift to other bases of status and citizenship?

We have envisaged a contraction of the field of organised employment and some shift away from the organised provision of services. There will be contrary pressures as new technology makes new services available. Prostheses which would enable the blind to "see", for example, would give organised employment not only to those who manufactured them but also to those who fitted and maintained them. But if we assume that only that will be organised which is not possible or greatly wasteful if left unorganised—i.e. that society's built-in preference will be for the unorganised—then organised employment must contract. Whether that results in a few devoting a lifetime to employment or many undertaking comparatively short periods or all putting in a number of regular hours or some mixture of these is a matter of choice. Some tasks will demand special skills and experience which cannot be widespread and will imply the career of a lifetime, although probably a shorter "lifetime" than our present 40 years. And we must remember too that the prosperity underpinning the freedom to undertake unorganised activities will continue to rest on the products of a highly organised sector. Who will do what in that sector? In principle that could be arranged along the lines of national service with all citizens directed for stated periods. While not impossible, I consider that unlikely; the values which will be required for the constructive use of free time are not readily compatible with such a *dirigiste* and bureaucratic solution. We should, I believe, expect to see a greater degree of preference, and preparation, for individual choice. Whatever the mechanisms involved, organised employment would become more voluntaristic. What effect would that have on the nature of organised work?

The consequences for organisations

It is of course always possible to find people who are willing to accept special kinds of discipline to which the majority are not subjected. Armies and police forces, so long as they require comparatively few recruits, can find them. But it is unlikely that the organised sector could impose conditions which deviated too far from those outside it; if entry were voluntary, employment would have to be attractive.

Let us turn aside for a moment to examine a community in which organised work is on a voluntaristic basis. The kibbutzim in Israel require from their members a work quota related to age in return for their privileges of membership, which include entitlement to all the necessities and many of the luxuries of life. Originally agricultural settlements, they are now mixed; almost all practise agriculture but most also have an industrial plant, some more than one. Some have to employ external labour, a practice they would like to end as it negates kibbutz values and gives them a bad conscience, because members, especially the young, appear reluctant to take factory jobs that have been shaped by their technology. The fact that the members own the factory, whose management is answerable to the elected committees of the kibbutz, has had little impact on the nature of jobs. As a consequence the kibbutz movements have begun to turn to job and organisational design to improve the quality of working life. A team skilled in the sociotechnical approach has been achieving quite satisfactory results. Of course the plants are comparatively small; few employ more than 50-70 workers. But the kibbutzim are as concerned with profitability as a private employer, and the reluctance to work in the traditionally designed plant is the reluctance of people who can directly relate the success of the plant to their own standards and conditions of life. To the extent that I can generalise from the case of the kibbutz, I would conclude that as work in organisations becomes more voluntaristic, so it will be necessary to provide jobs which offer satisfaction and autonomy.

Previous articles[8] have described new forms of work organisation designed to offer a high quality of working life. Pressure for them, as we have said, does not come primarily from the workforce. But the present workforce consists of people brought up to expect that they will have to take jobs in organisations and that organisations and jobs are what they are. Their acceptance will not be shared by generations who have been brought up to see work in a different light. Current efforts to improve the quality of working life help those who are best off. They do nothing for the unemployed nor for those working in the worst conditions; on the whole it is the good employer who even considers the new methods. It can indeed be argued that the efforts of good employers to improve the quality of working life of their employees and to contain cyclical fluctuations in activity, avoiding lay-offs and redundancies, actually transfer the worst jobs and the most intermittent, unsteady and unpredictable loads to a backward sector of jobbing firms and a secondary labour market of married women, handicapped workers and the otherwise vulnerable or marginal. It is just here that attention is needed during the transition from a society based on the expectation of full employment to one in which employment is no longer the normative channel for the distribution of material and moral resources. As the employment sector begins to shrink, partly through embracing the new technology, its conditions and rewards will improve—part of the price that is demanded by organised labour for agreement to technological change. The gap between those employed in the advanced sector and the rest, especially the unemployed, will widen. The advanced sector, as indicated above, will introduce improvements in the quality of working life because it depends on the commitment of those it employs. Tasks that do not appear to be improvable or for which the effort does not appear worth while will be contracted out to the backward sector. One possible scenario, often presented in this context, depicts an aristocracy of labour in the advanced sector with an army of helots outside it. As I see it, the advanced sector can indeed look after itself and during the period of transition will move in the direction which will be appropriate for the new order of things. I do not say it will need no help; just that it will seek that help of its own accord. I expect the advanced sectors of the service economy to follow the same pattern as the industrial, although with less ease and assurance. But can the same be said for the rest?

Almost by definition, the residual, backward sector of the service economy cannot be expected to undertake its own transformation. First, it is inadequately capitalised. Secondly, it is inadequately staffed with educated and trained managers. Thirdly, it is scantily unionised. Fourthly, it is far less likely to employ the kinds of consultant who could help. Furthermore, it is unlikely to be under pressure during the transition period. When people need employment which is relatively hard to find they will accept it without demanding such frills as participation. It will also take time for the firm which has not been able to consider the use of a computer to discover the possibilities that the minicomputer can offer it. However, it is probably just this sector which offers the greatest possible breakthrough for the minicomputer and where the greatest pay-off would come from its introduction.

Here, if anywhere, the capabilities of the new technology for centralisation and control or for decentralisation and participation are most marked. Here the mistakes that were made in the advanced sectors with the computer can be confidently expected to be repeated. But if they *can* be avoided the whole transition may be eased. One possibility for the future, for example, would be the development in the backward sectors of cooperatives whose members would undertake a certain number of hours' work. The fewer those hours, the more important it would be that members should be flexible and able to undertake a variety of tasks, the greater the value of self-managing teams, and the greater the need for smooth handover from team to team. With the aid of the minicomputer the complete state of the game could be made available by the outgoing to the incoming team, provided that members can both enter information into it and extract information from it. In this as in other ways microelectronics combines one of the benefits of centralisation (the complete picture) with the advantages of decentralisation (flexibility and self-management).

Another possibility is the cottage industry; much clerical and some blue-collar work could indeed be done by the individual at home, with a computer link to the centre making all relevant information immediately accessible. Asked whether they would welcome being able to work from home rather than going to office or factory, 35 per cent of a recent British sample was in favour and 59 per cent against; details were not given of any age differences, but women were somewhat more in favour than men. If self-selection for jobs were sufficiently free, it seems that there would already be enough people prepared to fill such home-based jobs as became available. And if jobs take up a small proportion of total time, any resulting social isolation may in fact be very slight.

Decentralisation, autonomy, self-management spread the functions of management but cannot take care of all co-ordinating and planning functions, let alone all research and development. And if top management is to learn its role, and if research and development are to prosper, will there not be need for some lifetime careers? Will we require a dedicated priesthood of technocrats separated from the rest of humanity? At present the road to the top is too long and too many of our institutions are gerontocratic. Little would be lost if careers were shortened. Some would prefer such careers even if they involved commitment to more of a lifetime spent in organisational employment than was the norm for others. And specialised planning and co-ordination, research and development are not incompatible with democratic forms of decision-making, provided they do not imply control. The technocrat as expert still has plenty of power, but not *controlling* power. This distinction weakens when he alone understands the issues. Then the expert is indeed on top rather than on tap. Some forecast that the new technology will divide us into those who understand and control it and those who are controlled by it, with no skills in between. Even if this is possible, it is not inevitable; the prophets have thought only of cognitive and manual, and ignored social, skills. They have assumed, as I have not, that no other change occurs. In high-process technology the need for the process worker to comprehend the process has become apparent and, with it, the advantages of multiskilled teams. The skills in decision-making and the team responsibility that goes with them can bridge the technocratic gap.

The role of labour unions

One institution that will come under increasing strain during the transition I have been describing is the trade union movement. Less concerned with quality of working life issues than with their fear of mass unemployment, which they see as the major threat, and adamant that workers' living standards be maintained, trade unions appear as the opponents of change. The remedies they propose are work sharing, expansion of employment through economic growth and, in each country, isolationist measures to avoid the export of jobs. In their espousal of work sharing and reduction of hours they are moving in what I consider the right direction. In urging the expansion of employment they are wrong for three reasons: first, there is no virtue in producing goods and services nobody needs or wants; secondly, resources of energy and materials need conserving; and thirdly and most importantly, as I have argued, there is no virtue in employment *per se.* The unions' problem is that they have attained their present form in a world where employment and employing organisations have been paramount, and they have two constituencies whose interests conflict—the employed who wish to preserve their living standards and the unemployed who want work. The unions can see perhaps better than anyone that lives are too precious to be wasted performing unnecessary activities all the hours of daylight, but like everyone else they are locked into a system where attendance at a place of employment is the only passport to full membership of society. And if employment became less important, then would the unions be less important too?

It is possible that the unions that survive the transition will be those that transfer their emphasis from their "industrial" role of negotiating pay and conditions and protecting the worker within the enterprise towards their "political" role of concern with issues of power, ownership and control and the conservation of resources. It will be their task to press for and obtain the fair sharing of power within the enterprise, the fair sharing of resources among those employed and those otherwise occupied. Above all they will have embraced the concept of the quality of working life as a means of sharing the organisational resources of power.

It seems more and more probable that the problems and opportunities presented by the new technology will transcend national boundaries. No country will be able to avoid its impact by exporting its problems, though some will try. Unions will be increasingly involved in international or supranational politics.

The changing role of industry

With the reduction in the hours and years of employment, the value of employment will weaken; it will be seen to be less valuable in itself.

Especially in regard to industry the question will become: what are you doing with this resource of man-hours? Paradoxical it may be, but I expect time to be valued more when it is plentiful than when it is scarce. When industry has little of people's time it will be under pressure to use it with care, to husband it. And the less time we give to an activity, the more we resent spending more.

Industry indeed will be under pressure to conserve all resources, human resources included, as society becomes more concerned with the future and more aware of global disparities, an awareness which the microprocessor will serve to increase by cheapening communication. Conserving both material and human resources will not be easy and will require novel solutions, some of which can already be seen approaching. The conservation of energy and of material resources argues for continuous plant operation. The conservation of human resources argues against shift working. Smart devices make virtually unmanned shift work a reality, allowing such labour-intensive activities as maintenance to be done on daytime shifts instead of at night and weekends.

Developments of this kind presuppose our adoption of more appropriate indicators than our present measures of profitability and productivity. There is no incentive to conserve resources if their cost represents the cost of their extraction and their present abundance rather than their future scarcity, a lesson now being learned in the case of oil. There is no incentive to reduce shift work if the premium paid for it is small compared with the social costs borne by the community. The easy way of dealing with such issues by legislation or by administered pricing has contributed to the distortion of values, continually preventing "profitability" from giving a true account of the services rendered to the community in exchange for the resources used. One effect of the microelectronic revolution is to make the search for better resources more urgent.

Consequences for developing countries

In this paper I have had little to say about the impact of microelectronics on developing countries. Advancing technology has hitherto tended to widen the gap between the developing and the developed. It has employed capital, which is scarce in developing countries, rather than labour, which is abundant. The labour it has required has been skilled and scarce rather than unskilled and abundant. It has enabled developed countries to find substitutes for the raw materials they would otherwise need to import from the developing countries, thus reducing their dependence upon them, except for oil. It has required an infrastructure of communications, and institutions abundant in the developed and scarce in the developing world. Will microelectronics follow the same pattern? Or will its potential for decentralisation apply here too? If cheap, easily used devices can monitor irrigation flows, test and adjust soil constituents, monitor and adjust the constituents of animal feed, cannot the yields of Third World agriculture be greatly enhanced? If the microprocessor makes possible the adoption of cottage industry methods, can some of the present disadvantages of poor infrastructure be overcome? So long as all the initiatives remain in the developed countries, it is unlikely.

* * *

In the course of this essay I have allowed myself some glimpses of a future which microelectronics makes possible. But is it probable? That depends on the choices that will be made in the near future. My fear is that those choices will be made under the wrong pressures, national pressures to obtain competitive advantage, pressures to maintain employment and create more. The choice will be made by politicians, industrialists, technocrats for whom the quality of life is measured by GNP and the quality of working life by the size of the pay packet. And these are bad times for taking the longer view.

Notes

[1] See Ronald Inglehart: *The silent revolution. Changing values and political styles among Western publics* (Princeton (New Jersey), University Press, 1977), p. 38.

[2] Ibid., p. 32.

[3] *British Public Opinion* (London), Autumn 1979.

[4] Op. cit., p. 46.

[5] Inglehart, op. cit., table 2-2, pp. 36-37.

[6] See Louis E. Davis: "Evolving alternative organisation designs: their sociotechnical bases", in *Human Relations* (New York), Vol. 30, No. 3, 1977, pp. 261-273.

[7] Pehr G. Gyllenhammar: *People at work* (Reading (Massachusetts), Addison-Wesley, 1977).

[8] See for example Davis, op. cit.

International Labour Review, Vol. 119, No. 6, November-December 1980

Settlement of labour disputes in essential services

A. PANKERT *

Introduction

Employers, workers and governments are generally agreed that some activities are of such importance for the community as to justify subjecting the settlement of labour disputes in these areas to special rules in order to limit the damage they can cause.

While it is simple for the parties concerned to agree upon this principle, it is often difficult for them to see eye to eye on the way it should be applied. The main problems consist, first of all, in defining the activities which should be governed by special rules and, secondly, in determining exactly how these rules should differ from the general system.

Although these are questions that have been raised since the dawn of industrialisation, they still crop up regularly in the debate on industrial relations. In many countries the existing rules, or the way they are applied, are the subject of frequent criticisms either on the part of the public, which finds them too permissive, or on the part of workers, who consider them too restrictive; as a result they are often applied with varying degrees of strictness and sometimes have to be modified.

This article aims to provide a general picture of the current situation as regards the settlement of labour disputes in essential services as well as of the most important trends and problems which have recently emerged in this field.

We shall be dealing solely with "interest" disputes (i.e. those which arise in the course of collective bargaining) and not with "rights" disputes (those concerning the application or interpretation of existing legal provisions or clauses in collective agreements). The reason for this is that in many countries rights disputes are in any event subject to the binding decision of a third party and consequently cannot result in strikes or lockouts.

* International Labour Office.

We shall not be examining the situation in the socialist countries with centrally planned economies since in these States industrial relations are conceived basically as a means of ensuring co-operation between management and workers with a view to implementing economic and social plans, and consequently as being incapable of generating any real clash of interests.

The basic problem

The basic problem in any system for the settlement of labour disputes in essential services arises from the fact that its ultimate objective must necessarily be to avoid prolonged interruptions—and sometimes even any interruption at all—in certain activities. This objective can of course only be attained by limiting the right of the employers and, more particularly, the workers involved to defend their interests through collective bargaining and recourse to direct action; at the very least there must be a possibility of limiting these rights in certain exceptional circumstances. The question, then, is one of trying to balance the general interest against the rights of the parties to the dispute. This involves establishing which services are in fact really essential and imposing on the rights of the parties only such limitations as are absolutely necessary.

For a long time it was thought that the arrangements made for settling labour disputes in essential services involved no major problems other than the one just cited. This is no longer the case. Gradually, over the years, the conviction has taken root in a growing number of countries that collective bargaining deserves to be protected and encouraged not only as a means whereby employers and workers may defend their particular interests, but also as an institution. In many quarters collective bargaining is even considered the most effective way of resolving labour problems and, as a result, the one most consonant with the general interest. It is clear, however, that provisions which are primarily designed to prevent the interruption of certain activities are bound quite often to hinder the collective bargaining process. Consequently it will be necessary to balance the advantages gained from the continuous functioning of essential services against the negative consequences these provisions may have not only for the right to bargain of the employers and workers concerned but also for collective bargaining as such.

The origin of the regulations

In the vast majority of countries the regulations applicable to labour disputes in essential services are the product of legislation. There are, however, a few countries, such as Sweden and the Federal Republic of Germany, which provide exceptions to this rule. In Sweden the problem is mainly regulated on the basis of an agreement between the parties. The Basic Agreement for the private sector provides that in the event of a dispute in an essential service the Labour Market Council, a joint body established at the national level, may, with the agreement of the majority of its members, recommend "preventing or settling a conflict" and propose "a consequent regulation of working conditions".[1] A similar system is provided for in the Basic Agreement for the public service. In the Federal Republic of Germany the principal text is the directives issued by the German Confederation of Trade Unions (DGB). Adopted in 1949 and amended in 1974, these provide inter alia that in the event of a labour dispute the workers should continue to perform the tasks necessary for safeguarding industrial installations and for supplying the population with essential goods and services.

It is not surprising that the majority of arrangements for settling labour disputes in essential services have a legal basis since they relate directly to the protection of the general interest which is primarily a prerogative of the public authorities.

Experience seems to show that the systems based on collective agreements or trade union directives are only possible in countries where there is a long tradition of industrial relations geared towards co-operation rather than confrontation and where workers are deeply committed to their trade unions.

The great advantage of the voluntary systems is that they have, by definition, obtained the assent of the trade unions. This is very important since it is well known that in this field it is practically impossible to impose solutions to which the vast majority of workers are firmly opposed. It might be recalled in this regard that legislation introduced in the United Kingdom in 1971 and in British Columbia in 1968—we shall return to these texts later—aroused such a hostile reaction from organised workers that it had to be repealed within a few years. Similarly, in Colombia, the inclusion of banks in the list of essential services in 1959 caused such vehement protests that it had to be revoked shortly afterwards. One could also cite many cases in which legal provisions prohibiting strikes in certain essential services have been contravened or where requisition orders issued against striking workers have in practice gone unheeded.

There have been very few new developments since the end of the Second World War as regards the source of regulations in this area, whether legislation, collective agreements or trade union directives. In any event there do not appear to be any countries which have radically changed their system in this respect during the postwar period. It should, however, be noted that in Italy, where the matter has traditionally been dealt with by legislation, the unitary CGIL-CISL-UIL trade union federation adopted in January 1980 a voluntary "code of conduct" on strike action, which will later be supplemented by specific measures for the various sectors and includes provisions concerning the continuous operation of essential services. It is still too soon, however, to say exactly what role these directives will play in the years to come.

The definition of essential services

The definition of the concept of essential services is a very important factor in any industrial relations system. Where the rules applicable to these services impose major limitations on the freedom of employers and workers, the effect of a relatively broad definition of the concept could be to give the entire labour relations system a somewhat restrictive character.

The situation has changed considerably in many countries over the last 20 or 30 years in regard to the number and nature of the activities considered to be essential.

Essential services and the public sector

The first notable development in this field has been in the public sector.[2] By this we mean all branches of wage employment in which the State is the employer or the sole or main proprietor, i.e. the civil service itself, parastatal bodies providing a public service (such as the railways and the postal, telegraph and telephone services) and state-owned agricultural, industrial or commercial undertakings.

Formerly industrial relations throughout the civil service and sometimes other parts of the public sector as well were often governed by extremely restrictive regulations, which were frequently justified—in part if not exclusively—by the argument that all the services provided were, by definition, essential. Regulations of this type are still fairly widespread. In many countries, both industrialised and developing, the entire civil service is still governed by dispute settlement machinery based on a prohibition of strikes and on compulsory arbitration. Sometimes these restrictions apply also to other parts of the public sector. Countries in this category include Colombia, where they extend to almost all state undertakings, and Japan, where they cover all "public corporations and national enterprises" (which are responsible, among other things, for running the railways, the postal, telegraph and telephone services and the production and retailing of salt, tobacco and alcohol).

The notion that the services provided by the public sector are all essential has, however, never met with universal acceptance. For some years now it has been noted more and more frequently that when the whole civil service, or even the whole public sector, is governed by special industrial relations rules the criterion applied is not the essential nature of the activities concerned but the legal nature of the employment relationship (under public or private law) or the identity of the employer (State or private person). It is in fact difficult to maintain that lower-level public servants working in a service of secondary importance—still less certain state undertakings—are performing really essential tasks. Hence it is not surprising that such countries as the United Kingdom, Norway, Malaysia and several French-speaking African countries have long since established distinctions between employees in the public sector according to the nature of their functions, or that a number of others—particularly among the industrialised countries—have recently adopted a similar approach. For example, Sweden in 1965 and Canada in 1967 lifted the ban on strike action, which had until then covered the whole civil service, while at the same time making provision for special rules governing the settlement of labour disputes in certain services regarded as genuinely essential. Similarly in Italy, where the 1931 Penal Code provides for penalties in the event of any strike in the civil service, decisions of the Constitutional Court in 1962 and 1969 had the effect of limiting the scope of that particular provision to strikes affecting activities considered to be truly indispensable.

The situation in the public sector has thus become much more akin to that in the private sector, where it is very widely accepted—at least as a matter of principle—that a special dispute settlement procedure should only be established in respect of services that are of a genuinely essential nature. What then is a "genuinely essential" service?

The meaning of "essential"

In seeking to define the essential nature of a service we are faced with two basic questions which are very closely linked and which for this reason may be dealt with together. The first, a question of form, is whether it is preferable to adopt a definition formulated in general and abstract terms or to enumerate the actual services it is intended to treat as essential. The second, a question of substance, is of course which activities should be regarded, explicitly or implicitly, as essential.

The enumeration method is used in a great many countries in Asia, Africa, Latin America and the Caribbean but it is less widespread in the other regions of the world. Countries using this system include Belgium, Brazil, Colombia, India, Jamaica, Kenya, Malaysia, New Zealand, Nigeria, Pakistan, Panama, the Philippines, Sierra Leone, Sri Lanka, Trinidad and Tobago, Venezuela and Zambia.

Although there are a number of differences in the composition of the lists drawn up in these countries, it is possible to make three general observations about them.

First, the majority of the services listed are concerned either with safeguarding industrial plant—by avoiding, for example, any stoppage of continuous process equipment—or with protecting the safety and health of the population. This second category mainly includes the armed forces and the police; the fire brigade; the public health and sanitation services; the production and distribution of basic foodstuffs, water, gas, electricity and some other sources of energy, such as petroleum products; transport and communications; and docks. Obviously there are cases where a stoppage of these activities, especially if it is not a complete one, does not strictly speaking affect the safety and health of the population but causes purely economic damage or just plain inconvenience. None the less, labour disputes in these services are as a rule apt to cause disruptions in the life of the community that can rapidly become dangerous.

Secondly, more and more countries have in recent years included in their list of essential services certain activities which are not concerned with safeguarding industrial plant or protecting the safety and health of the population but in which a prolonged interruption can cause very serious damage to the national economy. This trend is particularly noticeable in the developing countries. In Zambia, for instance, mining activities have been listed as essential services since 1971. The same applies to the cultivation, manufacture and refining of sugar in Trinidad and Tobago since 1972. In the Philippines, by virtue of Presidential Decree No. 823 of 1975, as amended, essential services include the production of sugar, textiles, clothing, certain articles classified as essential by the National Economic Development Agency and many goods destined for export. There has also been a move along the same lines in some industrialised countries. For example, in New Zealand (where meat exports play a major role in the economy) slaughterhouses operating for the export trade have been treated as essential services since 1976 whereas previously only those operating for domestic consumption were so regarded. It should be noted also that various countries, both industrialised and developing, have recently included in their list of essential services certain financial operations such as those carried out by banks and foreign exchange offices.

Thirdly, and contrary to what one might think, an enumeration of essential services does not necessarily impose a straitjacket on the authorities' freedom of manœuvre. In quite a few countries which have adopted this system the government has in fact been empowered from the outset to expand these lists by means of a highly expeditious procedure. In addition, besides the provisions applicable to the services listed as essential, many of these countries have other provisions of a very general nature enabling the government to intervene in any dispute which it sees as endangering the national economy or the national interest in general. In some countries possibilities of this type have existed for many years while in others they have only been introduced more recently. In Colombia, for example, the list contained in the Labour Code, which was limitative until 1956 but has since become merely illustrative, was supplemented in 1968 by a provision empowering the President of the Republic, following a favourable opinion of the Supreme Court, to put an end to any dispute "seriously affecting the interests of the national economy".[3] Similar provisions were introduced in Pakistan in 1974 and in Panama in 1976.

The degree to which the authorities have in practice added to the list of essential services or intervened in disputes arising in activities *not* included in this list varies greatly from country to country. While some governments have availed themselves of these powers extensively, others have never used them.

Concern for flexibility has of course always been particularly pronounced in countries which have rejected any enumeration of essential services and have confined themselves to a general definition. This is true, for example, of the United States, a number of European countries and several French-speaking African nations. Sometimes the legislature, despite its desire for a flexible system, has taken care to define essential services in a relatively narrow fashion. In the United States, for instance, the Taft-Hartley Act of 1947, which applies to all sectors of the economy with the exception of agriculture, the railways and air transport, provides that the special system governing the settlement of labour disputes in the case of "national emergencies" can only be applied when a dispute affecting "an entire industry or a substantial part thereof" will imperil "the national health or safety".[4] In many other countries the definitions are founded, however, on much less precise notions such as the "far-reaching social importance" of the dispute (in Denmark), "the public interest" (in Sweden) or "public law and order" and "the general interest" (in the Ivory Coast). One cannot really say that these are true definitions.

When a country has not defined what is meant by an essential service or has done so only in very general terms it is important to know how this notion is interpreted in practice. The tendency to interpret it broadly, which we have already noted in the countries which use lists, is also found in those which have opted for general definitions. In the United States, for example, the emergency procedure provided for in the Taft-Hartley Act has often been applied to disputes which did not really imperil "the national health or safety". An instance often cited in this regard is the application of this procedure to the steel strike of 1959 even though only 1 per cent of steel production was needed for purposes of national defence. In Denmark, too, where Parliament has intervened on various occasions over the past 50 years to put a stop to certain disputes deemed dangerous for the community (generally by transforming the conciliator's final proposals into law), it should be noted that the purpose of several of the interventions made during the 1970s has been to impose wage settlements where central negotiations had reached deadlock. It seems clear that these initiatives of the legislature were motivated more by economic considerations than by a desire to protect the safety and health of the population.

The above remarks enable us to make two series of comments concerning, respectively, the question of substance and the question of form raised by the definition of "essential".

As regards the question of substance, it might be asked whether it is a good thing that emergency procedures originally devised to safeguard industrial plant and protect the safety and health of individuals should now also be applied, in a growing number of countries, to disputes which seriously affect the national economy. To pose this question is not of course in any way to minimise the gravity of the problems caused by the latter type of dispute; it seems in fact that the question of the influence the authorities should (or should not) exert in the field of collective bargaining and the settlement of industrial disputes in order to help preserve or restore the major microeconomic balances is currently one of the most important in the whole field of industrial relations. It is certainly a question which has preoccupied the majority of developing countries since they gained independence and which the recession has brought to the forefront in many industrial nations. While there can obviously be no question here of laying down the law on how to resolve labour disputes that are likely to cause serious damage to the national economy, it is not unreasonable to suggest that a dispute of this nature differs too greatly from one in a hospital or power-station to be dealt with in the same fashion. At the very least, before resorting to a procedure designed for other situations, an effort should be made to ascertain that there are no better alternatives. Has the question really been gone into sufficiently deeply to know for certain that such alternatives do not exist?

As regards the question of form—and whatever the answer found for the question of substance—it seems that the problem of choosing between a list of essential services and a general and abstract definition of them is largely a false one. The fact is that many countries which originally opted for the listing procedure have subsequently taken powers that give them almost as much room for manœuvre as the countries without lists.

These developments seem to indicate clearly that a modicum of flexibility is indispensable in defining essential services. There are two reasons for this.

First of all, it is not certain that "essential" can be defined adequately through the enumeration of certain "activities". In the preamble to the Basic Agreement applicable in Sweden to the private sector the signatories declare that "a certain activity is rarely in itself of such fundamental importance to the community as to warrant its protection against any conflict" and that the repercussions of a conflict on the community depend as much on the extent of the conflict as on the nature of the activities affected. They conclude that "no other solution appears to offer itself than to permit the balancing of conflicting interests to assert itself in each individual conflict".[5] The same conclusion was reached in Canada (at the federal level) in 1968 by the Task Force on Labour Relations. Even if one is not prepared to push the argument as far as that, one can scarcely deny the validity of the considerations on which it is based.

The second reason militating in favour of flexibility is that it should be possible to take into account, in the application of the rules, a number of extrinsic factors which willy-nilly play a very important part. Is there any need to recall that the attitude adopted by the authorities to a labour dispute often largely depends on the limits to the public's patience or even on purely political considerations? It is these factors which explain why it has frequently happened in almost all countries that the disputes procedure established for essential services has been applied in the case of relatively harmless disputes while it has not been in the case of other much more serious ones.

It might be feared that the more imprecise the definition of essential the easier it would be to invoke this procedure. While this danger is not an imaginary one, it seems nevertheless that the frequency with which this procedure is used does not depend primarily on the precision with which essential services are defined. In Sweden, where there is no definition, the discussions held in the Labour Market Council in connection with major disputes have only once resulted in a real decision (in 1953 on the occasion of a dispute in privately owned electric power-stations). In the United States, on the other hand, the emergency procedure provided for in the 1926 Railway Labour Act (also applicable since 1936 to air transport) has been invoked more than 200 times, even though this Act applies to only two sectors of activity and contains a definition (of sorts) since it states that this procedure can be used only if a dispute should "threaten substantially to interrupt interstate commerce to a degree such as to deprive any section of the country of essential transportation service".[6] It seems therefore that the frequency with which recourse is had to the emergency procedures depends more on certain other factors and more particularly on the degree to which industrial relations in general are strained, since the less tense they are the fewer disputes there will be and the greater the number of those that can be settled through the ordinary procedure.

Dispute settlement procedures

Even more than the definition of essential services, the manner of settling disputes in these services raises many difficult problems. The relevant regulations vary considerably from country to country. Furthermore, recent trends in this field cannot always be reduced to a common denominator.

The present situation

The variety of existing systems for settling disputes in essential services is particularly marked in the industrial nations. Several partly overlapping distinctions can be drawn in this regard.

Firstly, we can distinguish between countries which are primarily concerned to find a satisfactory solution to the dispute and those which give priority to protecting the community against its harmful consequences.

For example, the rules applied in the Scandinavian countries are mainly designed to exhaust every possibility of conciliation. The same applies in the United States (at the federal level) where the Taft-Hartley Act of 1947 and the Railway Labour Act of 1926 both provide that the President may, in certain circumstances, order the postponement or interruption of a strike or lockout for a specified period during which particularly intensive efforts will be made to achieve an amicable settlement. In Japan, too, the accent is placed on conciliation and mediation, with the important reservation nevertheless that strikes are forbidden in public corporations and national enterprises and that the Government can submit disputes in these to arbitration. The position is different in Belgium and Portugal, where the principal concern of the legislator has been to ensure the partial operation of essential services by providing that part of the staff must remain at work. The same approach has been adopted in the above-mentioned directives of the German Confederation of Trade Unions and the code of conduct recently adopted in Italy. In France the major preoccupation of the legislator has also been to soften the impact of the dispute on the public. To this end the Government has been given extensive requisition powers which have, however, practically ceased to be used since 1963. An Act passed in that year, which applies to the civil service and to the staff of every public or private undertaking, body or establishment running a public service, requires that prior notice must be given of strike action and prohibits staggered or "rolling" strikes.[7]

Another distinction can be made between countries where the nature of the measures applied in the event of disputes in essential services is as a rule determined in advance in a relevant regulation and those in which it is generally only fixed on an ad hoc basis when a dispute arises. While countries like Belgium, France and the United States—whose systems have just been briefly described—belong rather to the first group, others such as the United Kingdom and Canada (federal level) belong to the second. Ad hoc measures applied in the United Kingdom consist mainly in the establishment of special commissions of inquiry or in recourse to emergency measures such as calling in servicemen to perform certain indispensable tasks. In Canada these measures often take the form of a law ordering a resumption of work and referring the settlement of the dispute to arbitration.

It is obvious that the above distinctions are far from being absolutely clear-cut. Most countries, although leaning heavily in each of the two fields concerned towards one or other of the possibilities mentioned, have nevertheless not completely ruled out the other. Thus the majority of countries focusing their efforts on conciliation have nevertheless adopted provisions to ensure that some particularly important activities—notably those aimed at safeguarding industrial plant—are never interrupted. In some of these countries, such as Denmark, Sweden and the United States, the legislator has sometimes even intervened in disputes affecting less vitally important activities to order a resumption of work and to dictate the terms of a settlement. Another—highly composite—solution is that provided for in the American State of Massachusetts by the so-called Slichter Law of 1947: this empowers the Governor, in the event of a dispute in an essential service, to choose among several options including mediation, an inquiry, securing partial operation of the service concerned, and the seizure of enterprises involved in the dispute. This system, besides allowing a choice between conciliation and the resumption of work, is also midway between a predetermined and an ad hoc procedure. Many experts consider that the uncertainty surrounding the choice the Governor will make under the terms of the Slichter Law has encouraged the parties in dispute to exhaust every possibility of negotiation before taking industrial action. In the opinion of the same experts the laws in force at the federal level, which leave no doubt at all as to the nature and timetable of the emergency procedure, have served on the contrary to inhibit collective bargaining. They contend that because the parties know that they risk nothing more than an inquiry and conciliation procedure and can foresee precisely how long it will last, they often begin to bargain seriously only when this procedure is completed, making use of it above all to strengthen their tactical positions in preparation for the final phase of the negotiations. This attitude is said to be particularly widespread in sectors such as the docks, where recourse to emergency procedures is relatively frequent.[8]

The great diversity of regulations applied in the industrialised countries does not prevent their having at least one point in common. Most of these countries, while not excluding recourse to coercion as an exceptional measure, nevertheless feel a certain repugnance towards it. This applies particularly to countries like Sweden and the Federal Republic of Germany, whose systems are essentially voluntary, but the other industrialised countries are also very much aware that constraint is inconsistent with their tradition of industrial relations and endeavour to avoid it as far as possible. This no doubt explains why they resort more and more rarely to such methods as compulsory arbitration, requisition, industrial conscription or seizure. In the United Kingdom it is even provided that conscription may never be used in the event of a proclamation of a state of emergency and that no other measure taken on such occasion may have the effect of turning the strike into a criminal act. In the Federal Republic of Germany it was recently laid down in the Constitution that the extraordinary measures which the authorities are empowered to take in certain national emergencies may not infringe the right to strike and to lock out, provided that this right is exercised in connection with economic or social questions.

In the developing regions the position is more homogeneous than in the industrialised world. Although the countries of Asia, Africa, Latin America and the Caribbean increasingly recognise the value of collective bargaining as a means of resolving economic and social problems, most of them have nevertheless deemed it necessary, in the interests of economic development, to establish fairly restrictive systems of labour dispute settlement for essential services. Apart from a few exceptions—like Mexico, which has limited itself mainly to taking certain measures in respect of notice of strike action and the safeguarding of industrial plant—most developing countries have introduced procedures for these services that are based on a prohibition of strikes and lockouts and on compulsory arbitration. Here and there these measures are automatically applied but in general it is up to the government to decide in each particular case whether or not to use them.

Recent developments

Changes that have occurred over the past 20 to 25 years in the procedures for settling labour disputes in essential services are both more fundamental and more of a kind in the developing countries than in the industrialised ones.

The systems involving compulsory arbitration and a ban on strike action that are in force in many developing countries are not always of long standing. In many cases they were adopted only in the 1960s to replace far less restrictive regulations dating from the colonial era. Most of the changes made since 1970 have no longer aimed to introduce a completely new system but to modify the existing rules—and practically all of them have resulted in a tightening up of the arrangements already in force. For example, the amendments to the Labour Codes of Senegal and Tunisia introduced in 1971 and 1973 respectively strengthened these Governments' hands by granting them certain powers of requisition, and new laws adopted in Nigeria in 1976 and in Sri Lanka in 1979 have considerably increased the penalties for trade unions and individual workers in the event of strikes in essential services.

The regulations currently applied in the industrialised countries are generally much older than those in the developing ones. Leaving aside some very recent developments whose real impact it is still too early to assess, such as the introduction in 1979 of a requisition system in Queensland and the adoption in 1980 in Italy of the code of conduct mentioned earlier, the dominant impression is that the majority of industrial nations have long been trying to avoid any fundamental reform in such a delicate area. It must be recognised, moreover, that the few attempts made in this field have generally not been encouraging. For example, the 1971 Industrial Relations Act in the United Kingdom, which laid down rules owing not a little to the Taft-Hartley Act of the United States, had to be repealed in 1974, and the 1968 Mediation Commission Act of British Columbia, which introduced an arbitration system, suffered the same fate in 1972. In these circumstances it is not surprising that recent changes in the industrialised countries have as a rule aimed only at making minor alterations to the existing schemes. These are too few and too varied to make it possible to identify any specific trend. Examples are the changes made in 1974 to the above-mentioned directives of the German Confederation of Trade Unions, whose principal object was to give greater autonomy to the affiliated national unions, or the amendments made in 1976 to the New Zealand legislation, the purpose of which was to introduce certain penal sanctions.

The United States and Canada occupy a special place among industrial nations in the sense that the settlement of labour disputes in essential services is the subject of more discussion and reforms than elsewhere. Numerous highly innovative proposals have been put forward in these countries at the federal level, of which one might mention the recommendations made in 1968 in Canada by the Task Force on Labour Relations and the Bill submitted in the United States in 1970 by the Nixon Administration concerning the transport sector. These two series of proposals, which were inspired by the Slichter Law of Massachusetts, provided that in the event of a failure of conciliation the competent authorities would have a wide range of options including the partial resumption of work and the submission of the dispute to an arbitrator. While ultimately neither country made substantial changes in the federal legislation, there has been no hesitation about launching a number of experiments in the Canadian provinces and the American states. In the years following the Second World War these experiments often concerned various forms of arbitration or seizure. Among the methods tested more recently is the "final offer selection" which has been adopted for, among others, the firemen and police of Wisconsin and Michigan. This is a type of arbitration in which the arbitrator must choose between the parties' final offers without being able to modify them. The aim is to encourage the parties to put forward reasonable proposals and thus promote collective bargaining. One might also mention as a curiosity that the "non-stoppage strike", which has been the subject of much comment in specialised American reviews, was used on several occasions in the United States during the 1960s. The object here is to reproduce as closely as possible a conflict situation (for example by depriving the workers of their wages and the undertakings of the profits made) without work being halted. The major difficulty with this technique is that it is practically impossible to recreate a situation similar in every respect to that produced by an actual work stoppage.

Summary and conclusions

As regards the definition of essential services, the idea that those provided by the civil service, or even the whole public sector, are all essential has been losing ground for some years. At the same time, there is a tendency to regard as essential not just the services primarily aimed at safeguarding industrial plant and protecting the safety and health of the population, but also those which are of great importance for the national economy. It is therefore becoming more and more difficult in an increasing number of countries to separate the problem of essential services, as it used to be understood, from that of the industrial relations role of the public authorities in protecting the interests of the national economy. As for the problem of the choice between listing essential services and defining them in a general and abstract way, it is often more apparent than real since many of the countries which originally opted for the first approach have subsequently adopted supplementary provisions giving their system almost as much flexibility as that which exists in other countries.

As regards the method of settling disputes in essential services, the developing countries have clearly tended in recent years to replace any less restrictive regulations with systems based on a prohibition of strikes and lockouts and on compulsory arbitration. The systems applied in the industrialised countries, which have not as a rule been significantly modified for many years, are both less coercive and more varied. Endeavouring to use constraint only in exceptional circumstances, these countries sometimes use pre-established procedures and sometimes ad hoc measures and put the accent, depending on the case, on conciliation or on protecting the public against the consequences of the dispute.

The diversity of labour dispute settlement systems in essential services confirms—if it were still necessary to do so—that there is no ideal answer to most of the major questions that arise in this field. To what extent can the authorities leave it to the employers and workers themselves to resolve the various problems raised by labour disputes in essential services? How can these services be defined sufficiently broadly and flexibly without at the same time leaving the door open for a massive, or even arbitrary, use of emergency procedures which could only undermine the effectiveness of such procedures? At what stage does it become necessary to call a halt, at least temporarily, to efforts aimed at settling the dispute amicably and to take coercive steps to secure the resumption of services paralysed by the dispute? Should the measures to be taken in the event of a dispute in essential services be laid down once and for all or should recourse be had also—or solely—to ad hoc measures? Most of these questions do not represent mutually exclusive alternatives. As a general rule the solutions adopted will only produce satisfactory results if they achieve an appropriate balance between conflicting demands. It is not possible to establish in the abstract where this point of balance lies. This largely depends on a whole series of extremely variable factors including, first and foremost, the general characteristics of the national system of industrial relations and, more fundamentally, the political and economic conditions as well as the traditions and values which hold sway in the country concerned.

Notes

[1] Chapter V, article 3. The text of this agreement is reproduced in ILO: *Basic agreements and joint statements on labour-management relations*, Labour-Management Relations Series No. 38 (Geneva, 1971), pp. 168-186. This agreement has now been denounced and is being renegotiated, although with the agreement of both parties the chapter on the settlement of labour disputes in essential services remains in force.

[2] For further details on this subject see J. Schregle: "Labour relations in the public sector", in *International Labour Review*, Nov. 1974, pp. 399 ff.

[3] Act No. 48 of 1968, s. 3, para 4.

[4] S. 206. See *Legislative Series* (Geneva, ILO), 1947—USA 2.

[5] Idem: *Basic agreements and joint statements*. . ., op. cit., p. 171.

[6] S. 10. See *Legislative Series*, 1926—USA 1.

[7] Ss. 1, 3 and 4. See ibid., 1963—Fr. 1.

[8] See in particular J. T. Dunlop and D. A. Wells: *Procedures for the settlement of emergency disputes*, International Conference on Automation, Full Employment and a Balanced Economy, Rome, June 1967, pp. 3-4; H. W. Arthurs: *Labour disputes in essential industries*, Task Force on Labour Relations, Study No. 8 (Ottawa, Queen's Printer, 1968), pp. 132-142, 151-155, 228-232 and 237-239 and references; and K. W. Wedderburn: "Industrial action, the State and the public interest", in B. Aaron and K. W. Wedderburn (eds.): *Industrial conflict: a comparative legal survey* (London, Longman, 1972), p. 354.

International Labour Review, Vol. 119, No. 6, November-December 1980

Women's employment in France: protection or equality?

Marcelle DEVAUD and Martine LEVY *

Introduction

In declaring that the law guarantees women equal rights with men in all fields, the Preamble to the French Constitution of 1946 at last granted all French women the full citizenship rights of which they were still deprived despite the many struggles of the preceding decades. This constitutional guarantee ran counter to the legal provisions then in force, which stemmed from the Napoleonic Code and were based on a conception of women as beings who were incapable in law, dependent and in need of protection, whether in the family, at work or in society in general.

Thirty years later women have a totally different image characterised by the independence they have acquired through extended schooling, the exercise of an occupational activity, their ability to control procreation, more egalitarian marriage laws and a new political role. The problem is no longer one of putting new legislation on the statute book, since over the past few decades the law has already been largely brought into line with the aspirations voiced by women; what has to be done now is to work towards the practical realisation of the goal represented by equality of opportunity and treatment for men and women in our society [1] and, in particular, in working life.

The elimination of every kind of discrimination has thus become an obligation imposed on the international plane [2] and accepted at the national level. [3] As of now, the changed status of women calls into question—in the name of equality—the various forms of protection they have inherited from the past.

In the first part of this article we shall examine this inheritance to see how it originated and how it has evolved over time. In the second part we shall take stock of the protective or special measures which still remain following the pruning process carried out over the past ten years or so. The third part will summarise the various attitudes adopted by the main

* President and General Secretary, respectively, of the French Committee on Women's Work.

employers' and workers' organisations towards these protective measures, as well as the proposals contained in an official report. The final section will sum up the consensus reached on this question by the Committee on Women's Work in its dual concern to guarantee women equality of opportunity and treatment with men while at the same time preserving their acquired rights in respect of maternity.

1. The legacy of protective legislation

There were a number of reasons for the introduction in the nineteenth century of special legislation to protect working women, the most important of which were:

— the degrading conditions in which women were employed and the resulting dangers for their offspring; and

— the inferior status of women in society and the discrimination to which they were subjected by a large section of the trade union and socialist movement.

Degrading conditions of employment

The industrial boom in the second half of the nineteenth century led to the creation of much new employment. Women were soon called upon to supplement the male workforce and to take on wage-earnings jobs; it was not long before they constituted a sizeable proportion of the economically active population. Concentrated at first in the clothing industry, they were soon to be found working everywhere, including the mines and even as railway labourers in the Landes. "In the refineries the night-time unloading of sugar-beet will be carried out by women since they are more dexterous and supple than men and because they are better able to withstand mud and cold", states a circular issued by the Northern Refineries in 1860.

In 1851, despite the importance of home work, where women predominated, 39 per cent of the manual workers employed in large-scale industry were women. Having no vocational training, women were employed on the hardest and most menial tasks. "One sees women pickers and carders condemned to live amidst thick clouds of dust while male spinners and piecers breathe freely in large well ventilated rooms", wrote Adolphe Blanqui in his description of the workshops in Lyons. Throughout France women in the textile industry worked in premises that were as hot as ovens or as cold and damp as cellars.

The health situation was deplorable. For example, in the case of lacemakers, who started work at the age of 6, "half at least are affected by one of many eye infections such as engorgement of the eyelids, myopia or blindness caused by extreme fatigue of these organs". In 1873 Leroy-Beaulieu published a survey on women workers in which he wrote: "One cannot count the number of cases of spontaneous abortion, premature births, poisoning, ophthalmia, 'cotton-dust asthma', menstrual disorders and silicosis caused by working conditions." On the one hand, however, these were not officially recognised as occupational illnesses and diseases and, on the other, it was always up to the woman to furnish proof of her employer's negligence.

Under the Second Empire the duration of the working day varied between 12 and 17 hours with an average of 15. Nursing mothers had to feed their children at night or sometimes during the mid-day break if they could find a neighbour to bring the baby to them. Infant mortality was already high and working conditions such as these for mothers could only make it worse. The cry was therefore raised for legislative intervention.

The inferior status of women[4]

Since the promulgation of the Napoleonic Code women had been regarded as legally incapable and assimilated to minors placed under the authority of men, be they fathers or husbands; it was only logical therefore that this authority, including moral authority, should have been entrusted to the employer inasmuch as women left the home to go to work and the hierarchy of the undertaking reproduced, as it were, that of the family. In addition there was a certain mistrust of women, which found expression in all the philosophical and political thinking of the day and was based on an inegalitarian conception of the sexes backed up by the theories of Proudhon about the physical and moral frailty of women.

Hence working women were the victims of a twofold discrimination: on the part of the employer, since their wages were never more than half those of men, and on the part of the emerging trade union movement. Jules Simon noted in *L'ouvrière* (1863) that women were excluded from most of the mutual aid associations set up to alleviate the harmful consequences of poor working conditions and unemployment. And even when they were admitted, their contributions were higher and, in the event of illness, they were only entitled to a doctor and medicines while men also received a cash benefit.

It was against this background that there came into being the notion of a secondary income (which women did not have free disposal of until the Act of 1907), a notion that is founded on the concept of the man as head of the family and provider of the household resources of which the woman/mother is the guardian in the home.

The introduction of protective legislation

Measures specially designed to protect the female workforce were adopted and amended in successive stages; workers' organisations gradually came to see the laws adopted for the protection of women and children as constituting a social advance and as a provisional victory pending the extension of the rights so acquired to the entire population.

19 May 1874. The employment of children under the age of 12 in manufacturing is banned. The working day is limited to 12 hours. The employment of women in mines and quarries, and of girls under the age of 21 on night work, is prohibited.

2 November 1892. The minimum age of admission to employment is raised to 13 years. The working day is limited to 10 hours for girls under the age of 16; and to 11 hours for adult women; weekly hours of work may not exceed 60. A weekly rest day and observance of legal holidays are recommended. The ban on night work is extended to all women in industry.

This same law equated the working woman to a minor of less than 18 years since section 16 provided that the heads of industrial and commercial establishments employing young workers under 18 years of age *and women* had to see to it that accepted standards of good behaviour were maintained and that public decency was observed. Numerous regulations were adopted in application of this law.

1900. Health and safety measures in workshops are provided for by law.

31 December 1900. The so-called "seats law". In every commercial establishment the employer is obliged to provide as many seats as there are female employees.

1902. The working day is reduced to 10½ hours for women and children.

1904. The working day is reduced to 10 hours for women and children.

28 December 1909. Pregnant women are granted eight weeks' maternity leave (without pay), during which time employers may not terminate their contracts of employment. The same decree (section 234-6 of the Labour Code) also fixes limits to the weights which may be carried, drawn or pushed by women and children.

1910. Women schoolteachers are granted maternity leave on full pay.

1911. So are women employed in the postal, telegraph and telephone services.

1913. The law prohibits a "woman who is recovering from her confinement" from being employed on arduous work. A decree regulates the conditions of employment in stalls outside shops, assimilating women, whatever their age, to male minors of less than 18 years of age (section R.234-4).

1915. A minimum wage is laid down for women homeworkers.

1922. Postal, telegraph and telephone employees work one hour less as from the sixth month of pregnancy.

1924. The so-called "Strauss law" provides that a pregnant woman on leave shall receive an allowance from the *commune*, varying according to the husband's income.

4 February 1928. The working day for nursing mothers is reduced by one hour for a period of one year. The employer must make suitable space available for them, and provide nursing rooms in undertakings employing more than 100 women.

1928. Maternity leave on full pay is extended to the entire public service.

Hence at the end of the last century and the beginning of the present one a body of legislation had been established to alleviate the worst constraints placed upon women by the working conditions of the time and, above all, to combat the harmful effects of these conditions on pregnancy and especially on the frequency of premature births and their after-effects.

Following the work done by Adolphe Pinard and the survey carried out by Professor Robert Debré in 1933 for the League of Nations, attempts were made in numerous studies, notably those of the National Institute of Health and Medical Research,[5] to assess the effectiveness of the protective provisions. The most recent dates from 1979[6] and describes the many improvements brought about by the Act of 1966 and, especially, since 1975.

In fact, the division of the Labour Code relating to maternity protection and the upbringing of children (sections L.122-25 to L.122-32) has been amended each year since 1975. The main changes were effected by Act No. 75-625 of 11 July 1975, which is basically designed to strengthen maternity protection but in such a way as not to undermine equality of the sexes. The report relating to the Bill drew attention, moreover, to the new inequalities which overly protective legislation could introduce: "To go any further in protecting pregnancy", it said, "could do young women more harm than good by leading some employers to decline systematically to recruit them."[7]

According to Michel Hardouin, "the law alone seems capable of restoring a balance which nature sometimes ignores. Regarded as a state of weakness, pregnancy calls for the protection of women; regarded as a constraint, it calls for their liberation."[8] He shows how the recent legislation is based on a new concern to ensure that women's rights take precedence over the employer's will. Pregnancy, whether a present fact or just a future possibility, must no longer be an obstacle to freedom to work. Guaranteed employment is becoming a central objective even if the safeguarding of workers' health retains its importance.

2. Protection of women at work: the present situation

The "privileges" or "advantages" (as some still consider them) enjoyed by women at work have been substantially reduced over the past decade, doubtless as a result of the general improvement in working conditions. However, some recent provisions in contract law appear to generalise and strengthen measures that will ensure increasingly effective maternity protection.

The pruning of protective measures

The elimination of a number of protective measures regarded as inconsistent with new trends in social behaviour and common law[9] is inspired by the desire to abolish all forms of discrimination against women.

J. M. Combette, technical adviser to the Secretariat of State for the Status of Women, concedes that any legislation or regulations repealing a social measure may appear to constitute a backward step, but points out that governments have to take the following considerations into account:

> To keep outdated measures on the statute book, even if they were fully justified in the past, would be to give implicit sanction to a discriminatory difference in treatment which could only be to the disadvantage of the category one is supposedly protecting. If the protective regulations no longer have any justification, they should be repealed. This is after all the normal fate of laws which have become obsolete.
>
> Equality between men and women in the area of employment does not of course mean parity but, apart from a few exceptions mainly relating to maternity—which anyway only concerns women during a certain stage of their lives—nothing should nowadays prevent a woman having access to the same jobs as men.[10]

It is difficult to demand equality of remuneration if (unjustified) prohibitions are retained on the statute book. Promoting the right of women to work therefore entails above all eliminating the various types of legal discrimination between men and women which remain in some fields of occupational life.

It was these considerations that inspired the drafting of section 7 of the Act of 11 July 1975 and of the Decree of 5 August 1975, which repealed or amended the previous legislation stemming from the Act of 2 November 1892 with a view to promoting equality of opportunity and treatment in employment. The same holds true for the Act of 2 January 1979, which modifies the scope of the ban on night work for women.

These various changes are based essentially on recognition of the independent status of the adult woman, which is now comparable to that of a man. The following are some examples:

- deletion of the provisions in section L.234-1 of the Labour Code respecting the employer's moral guardianship over adult women;
- the repeal of the provisions in section R.234-2 prohibiting the employment of women in the production or sale of writings, drawings, etc., whose sale is subject to strict controls as being liable to offend morality;
- the repeal, in respect of adult women, of the prohibition contained in section R.234-8 on employment in the repair of machines, mechanical appliances or parts in motion.

These last measures were originally designed to shield the most vulnerable categories of workers—vulnerable mainly because of their lack of skill—from the dangers resulting from the mechanisation of industry. Besides, the prevention of occupational hazards had not then reached the level of effectiveness we know today and consequently it was felt that only specially qualified workers should be employed on jobs regarded with good reason as being dangerous. Nowadays, the continued existence of such a prohibition might exclude certain women from well paid and attractive maintenance jobs. Henceforth, if they so desire, they can do the same jobs as men; this is the main contribution made by the removal of the protective measures.

The same applies to skilled women able to occupy responsible positions in industrial undertakings who are no longer excluded (in law at any rate) from a number of technical supervision jobs. In accordance with the exclusion clause in the Night Work (Women) Convention (Revised), 1948 (No. 89), they are no longer covered by the ban on night work. Even if for reasons of personal convenience there are perhaps not many of them who seek to take advantage of this opportunity, the fact remains that they cannot now be kept out of certain occupations on the ground that they might have to be on duty at night outside their home.

Other safety regulations have also had their scope reduced. For example, section R.234-4 of the Code concerning employment in outside stalls has been amended: from now on such work is prohibited for adult women after 10 p.m., when the temperature is below freezing-point, when they are pregnant, or when a doctor deems it necessary. As for section R.234-6 concerning maximum weights, it now provides that transporting weights with tricycles, pedal-driven carriers, etc., is prohibited only for pregnant women and women for whom a doctor deems it necessary. Otherwise women of 18 years and over are permitted to transport by such means a weight of up to 75 kilograms, the vehicle included.

Protective provisions

As a result of the developments mentioned above there remain few "special provisions for women" in respect of health and safety. Most of the remaining provisions, according to the list in Jacques Baudoin's report,[3] seem to be explicitly or implicitly concerned with maternity protection. However, there also seem to be a number of measures aimed at protecting the family and domestic role of women.

Explicit maternity protection

The provisions explicitly aimed at maternity protection include the following:

— a woman may not be dismissed during her pregnancy and for a period of 14 weeks following her confinement (extended by two weeks if she is delivered of more than one child) (section L.122-25-2 of the Labour Code);

— a woman is entitled to maternity leave on 90 per cent of her pay for 16 weeks (six before and ten after the confinement) (sections L.298 C of the Social Security Code and L.122-26 of the Labour Code);

— pregnant women may not be employed in stalls outside shops and stores after 10 p.m. or when the temperature is below freezing-point (section R.234-4 of the Labour Code);

— pregnant women may not transport weights by tricycle, pedal-driven carriers, trolleys or hand-carts (section R.234-6 *in fine*);

— special provisions regulate the temporary assignment of pregnant women to other posts (section L.122-25-1);

— women wishing to breast-feed their children on work premises are granted one hour per day during working hours and in certain cases the employer must provide a nursing room (sections L.224, L.224-b, R.224-1 and R.224-3).

Implicit maternity protection

Here the measures are not specifically aimed at pregnant women but may be regarded as serving to protect a pregnancy which has not yet been confirmed or which a woman, as is her right, does not wish to declare, especially during a probationary period. They include the following:

— the ban on the employment of women in underground work in mines and quarries (section L.711-3) and, especially, all the provisions prohibiting women from performing certain jobs or their regular access to premises used for processes regarded as dangerous or unhealthy (sections R.234-9 and R.234-10);

— maximum limits on weights according to sex (although a number of provisions, notably in the public and semi-public sectors, have recently lowered the limits for *both* sexes);

— the employer's obligation to provide in shops and stores a number of seats equal to the number of women employed therein (section R.232-36);

— the ban on the use of certain means of transport by women only, where a doctor deems it necessary (section R.234-6).

Protection of the family and domestic role of women

In the view of Monique Chaudron,[11] "labour law basically only recognises the family through the special status it confers on women. It thus reproduces a sexual distribution of roles in which the woman is equated with the family." The provisions protecting the domestic and family role of women mainly concern working time. They can be classified under the following headings:

Hours of work:

— limited to ten hours per day for women, with a break of at least one hour during which no work may be done (section L.212-9 of the Labour Code);

— ban on night work (i.e. between 10 p.m. and 5 a.m.) for women in industrial establishments except when authorised, in certain circumstances, by the Labour Inspectorate (sections L.213-1 ff.);

— grant of two days' additional paid leave per dependent child for women under 21 years of age (section L.223-5).

Work organisation:

— the ban on women doing shift work except in factories which have to operate continuously and in establishments designated by a government regulation (section L.212-11).

Retirement age:

— Act No. 75-1279 of 30 December 1975, which came into force on 1 July 1976, provides for retirement at 60 for female manual workers who are mothers of families;

— Act No. 77-774 of 12 July 1977 extended the possibilities of retiring at 60;

— in the public service, mothers with three or more children may retire after 15 years of service whatever their age.

Nevertheless, a trend has emerged towards establishing a link between the family and men or, rather, working fathers. For example, a father now has the right to three days' leave on the birth of a child; and if he loses his job he has priority in being allocated a new one. The Act of 12 July 1977 relating to parental leave provides that, if the mother waives her right, the father is entitled to take leave without pay for two years with the right to reinstatement in his job at the end of the leave and retention of his acquired rights. The new provisions concerning post-natal leave introduce the same entitlement into the public sector, and some collective agreements have transformed the termination of the employment contract because of post-natal leave into a mere suspension.

This legal innovation, which is fully in keeping with the law on parental authority and the gradual public acceptance of a greater sharing of roles between the marriage partners and within the family, has not yet been incorporated in all collective agreements. These seem to have taken over from the law in according special treatment to women, often with happy results when they improve the conditions under which pregnant women work. Thus article 10 of the skeleton agreement of 17 March 1975 provides that pregnant women shall benefit from rearrangements of working hours to be determined for each occupational branch. In the agreements concluded in the petroleum industry, chemicals, insurance, banks, department stores and the food industry, for example, one finds provisions concerning reduced daily hours of work, more flexible work schedules, rest breaks and free compulsory medical examinations. Numerous agreements guarantee women continued payment of their remuneration, particularly if it is above the ceiling, during maternity leave and even when this is extended on account of a pathological condition or by nursing leave.

Many agreements also provide special advantages in the sense that they offer women the possibility of working shorter hours in order to cope with their family duties[12] and particularly to look after their children when they are sick.

Hence the trends seem to be contradictory or at least equivocal. This impression would be even stronger if case law were taken into account: some decisions of the Court of Cassation seem to be lagging behind the law in this regard. This rather confused situation is surely the result of the diversity—and sometimes the divergence—of the attitudes adopted on this subject by the social and economic interest groups and a reflection of the different situations and often contradictory aspirations of the many categories of women.

3. Conflicting attitudes to protective measures: equality or protection?

When the social partners were consulted on the proposals made in the Baudoin Report[3] and on the European Community questionnaire relating to the implementation of equality of treatment for workers, the most representative employers' and workers' organisations adopted clear-cut positions, which we shall now attempt to summarise.

The proposals of the Baudoin Report

The Report attached great importance to updating the law and a large number of the proposals it contained concerned the revision of certain obsolete provisions involving so-called "positive" discrimination. Its aim was to eliminate the differences in the treatment of men and women so that the fact of belonging to one or the other sex should no longer have any relevance in the employment market.

Accordingly, the proposal was made to repeal section L.212-11 of the Labour Code concerning the prohibition of shift work, as well as sections

R.234-4 and R.234-6 concerning the ban on women, and only women, performing certain jobs if the industrial medical officer so advises. The point here is that section D.241-14 requires *all* employees to undergo a medical examination and provides that the industrial medical officer must judge whether an employee is fit for the work in question, separate provision being made for the protection of pregnant women. It is therefore superfluous to provide special protection for women on these various points except in respect of maternity.

Other proposals were aimed at eliminating any reference to sex in section R.232-30 (the "seats law"); revising, in the light of scientific advances, the schedule of processes prohibited to women because of presumed dangers in the event of as yet unconfirmed pregnancy (particularly in sections L.711-3, R.234-9 and R.234-10); and giving employees of both sexes the right to retire at the same age.[13]

The employers' position

This was clearly expressed by the representatives of the National Council of French Employers (CNPF); they sought the revision and adjustment of the regulations which create barriers to the development of women's employment, especially as regards outdated forms of protection, the rules governing night work and the rearrangement of working time.

The CNPF considered that the lifting of the ban on night work for women would be compatible with ILO standards on equality of opportunity and treatment, but it remained categorically opposed to the fixing of general limits on night work as well as to any moves which would limit recourse to night work save with a view to ensuring the necessary protection of children, adolescents and pregnant women.

The CNPF argued that special measures meant higher costs for the undertakings and could obstruct the advancement of women.

The unions' position

The General Confederation of Labour (CGT)

The CGT considered it necessary to bear in mind the reasons for the present situation and at the same time to attempt to change it: it could not be denied that the current social realities still called for protective measures.

As regards night work, it was against the lifting of the ban laid down in the legislation because of the types of jobs done by women in industry.

Despite what it considered a general improvement in working conditions, the CGT believed that technological progress permitted even greater advances and that the relevant laws and regulations should be strengthened in consequence.

It was in favour of the revision of certain obsolete provisions but considered that such revision should encompass all aspects simultaneously: eliminating outdated provisions, extending to men the protection granted to women workers, and considering the introduction of new special provisions for women adapted to the demands of modern life.

As regards the existing legislation, the CGT approved the removal of any reference to sex such as appears in section R.232-30; it was against the repeal of sections R.234-4 and 234-6 and hoped that the revision of the schedule of prohibited processes for women (sections L.711-3, R.234-9 and R.234-10) would not entail deletions but that the ban would be extended to male workers. It considered, moreover, that these prohibitions, being so few in number, did not create a real barrier to the greater access of women to an occupational activity.

As for the age of retirement, the CGT considered that in the present situation any woman worker should have the right, on request, to retire five years before the pensionable age of a male worker and without any reduction in her pension.

The CGT considered finally that for the time being all forms of payment by results should be prohibited for pregnant women and that they should continue to receive their remuneration in full.

The French Democratic Confederation of Labour (CFDT)

The CFDT wanted the ban on shift work to be maintained. It felt this was necessary and even deserved to be extended at a time when men and women workers were aspiring to a fuller say in the way their lives were organised.

As regards the sections of the Labour Code relating to maximum weights, the CFDT would have liked similar provisions to be applied to men in so far as technological progress permitted, which seemed possible in the majority of cases. It approved the revision of sections R.234-9 and R.234-10 concerning underground work.

For the CFDT the important thing was to adopt a revision procedure which would permit the drawing up of standards to ensure the protection of both men and women where there was a presumption of risk.

As regards the retirement age, the CFDT wanted it lowered for all, men and women alike; it recognised that this would necessitate a reform of many retirement schemes.

The French Confederation of Christian Workers (CFTC)

The CFTC could not agree that certain forms of so-called positive discrimination should be abolished in the name of blind egalitarianism: women workers were seeking equality in the sense of social progress and not a worsening of the constraints under which they lived. They could not accept attempts to abolish certain benefits which they had won with such difficulty. The CFTC reaffirmed its support for the ban on night work, which it wished to see extended to men except in a very few cases. It was also against changes in the hours of work fixed by law. On the other hand, it favoured greater flexibility in timetables (personalised schedules, flexible working day, etc.), of which women would be the prime beneficiaries because of their family obligations. But it considered that part-time work—an option available to women under some collective agreements—should never be compulsory.

The CFTC wanted all workers to be allowed the opportunity of taking individual leave for reasons of personal convenience at any time during their working life. It also thought it would be useful to extend to all workers some of the provisions currently applicable only to women (medical examination, seats, etc.).

The General Confederation of Labour-Force Ouvrière (CGT-FO)

The CGT-FO was very much in favour of strengthening the protection of pregnant women, extending to men certain provisions concerned with the care of children and increasing the resources earmarked for women's training.

It sought an updating of the Labour Code to eliminate obsolete provisions concerning the protection of working women and considered that the best protection for them lay in vocational and trade union training which would enable them to defend themselves against discrimination on equal terms with men.

* * *

To sum up, the various positions adopted by the organisations involved reveal a common concern to protect pregnancy and maternity, if necessary by improving the existing provisions.

While all the trade union organisations uphold the general principle of extending protection against hazards to both sexes, marked differences remain in regard to the importance they attach to the traditional family role of women and this no doubt reflects the views of the majority of their active members.

More particularly as regards night work and the discrimination associated with it—an issue widely debated at the present time both nationally and internationally—the unions consider that the protection guaranteed by ILO Convention No. 89 must be maintained and that new standards should be adopted for all workers regardless of sex and branch of activity.

Conclusion

Hand-in-hand with the shifts that have taken place in public attitudes and behaviour over the past century or so, the legislation concerning women's work and, especially, the protection of working women has undergone some radical changes.

Women workers, drawn largely from the reservoir of rural labour, were indispensable for the rapid expansion of industry in the second half of the nineteenth century. But they were completely at their employer's beck and call and were subjected in France (as in most other major industrialised countries) to extremely harsh working conditions. Systematically assigned to the hardest and nastiest jobs, women and children became the veritable slaves of modern times.

A number of legislators—socialist deputies and others influenced by Christian social thinking—soon became sensitised to this particularly inhumane situation, which for many young women was aggravated by the disorientation experienced by country folk totally at a loss in big cities. This humanitarian concern was soon reinforced by a fundamental concern for the preservation of the species. Earlier on we drew attention to the tragic consequences of interminable hours of work in unhealthy factories, e.g. spontaneous abortions, premature births and stillbirths.

This dual concern, and perhaps also the realisation that the very existence of this necessary workforce was at risk, inspired, as we have seen, a series of protective laws which, improving with the years, formed in the course of a few decades a by no means negligible body of social legislation for the benefit of working women.

The trade unions, sometimes after a little hesitation, rapidly perceived the value of these reforms not only for the women who were their immediate beneficiaries but also for male workers, who were able to use some of these provisions as a springboard to improved working conditions for themselves.

Today, a century later, working conditions have changed and the status of women has altered even more radically. While practice is admittedly not always identical with the law, the legal position is that women now enjoy total equality with men whether in respect of matrimonial status or as regards access to education, training or employment. They now possess the means of controlling pregnancies. And their role in national development is more indispensable than ever.

Consequently it must now be asked to what extent protective provisions are still justified and do not infringe the broad principle of non-discrimination, one of the most outstanding expressions of which is the Convention on the Elimination of All Forms of Discrimination against Women, adopted by the General Assembly of the United Nations in December 1979 and signed by France at the Copenhagen Conference last July.

While the role of the woman is inseparable from that of the mother and it is difficult to think of one without the other, it is nevertheless valid to divide maternity into what might be called the period of exclusively maternal activity (pregnancy and confinement), which annually affects approximately 6 per cent of working women, and the period of family activity, which involves looking after children until they reach adulthood. For the fact is that only the period in which the woman is expecting and finally gives birth is truly a special time requiring specific maternity protection measures. Maternity as a social function must be socially protected and the function of procreation justifies exceptional protective measures. As far as looking after children and other family obligations are concerned, these certainly call for protection but this should benefit fathers as well as mothers since family responsibilities should normally be shared between the parents.

This is the position adopted by the French Committee on Women's Work. It is also the way that the thinking behind French labour law seems to have been evolving over the past few years: to protect women in their procreative functions; to protect parents in carrying out their responsibilities, which in the past were traditionally assigned to the mother alone and henceforward must be shared; in employment, to protect those workers who appear to be weakest but especially to reduce hazards to the greatest possible extent, if they cannot be eliminated altogether; and to reorganise the arrangement of working time for all so that male and female workers alike can reconcile the obligations of their occupational activity with those of their family life.

Finally, for the future, the objective is to ensure that technological progress, which is already bringing about profound changes in the organisation of work and will do so even more between now and the end of the century, steadily reduces the burden on workers of both sexes and promotes their full personal development.

Notes

[1] See Secrétariat d'Etat à la Condition féminine: *Projet pour les femmes — 1976/1981* (Paris, 1975).

[2] EC Council Directive of 9 February 1976 on the implementation of the principle of equal treatment for men and women as regards access to employment, vocational training and promotion, and working conditions. See *Official Journal of the European Communities* (Luxembourg), No. L 39, 14 Feb. 1976, pp. 40-42.

[3] See Jacques Baudoin: *Les discriminations et les disparités dans le travail féminin*, report submitted to Robert Boulin, Minister of Labour and Participation, and Nicole Pasquier, Secretary of State for Female Employment. Pour une politique du travail, No. 15 (Paris, ministère du Travail et de la Participation, 1979).

[4] See Madeleine Guilbert et al.: *Travail et condition féminine*, annotated bibliography published in collaboration with the CNRS (Paris, Editions de la Courtille, 1977).

[5] Unpublished note by P. Lazar concerning the protection of pregnancy, 1978.

[6] Pierre Cabanes: *Maternité et travail*, report submitted to Robert Boulin, Minister of Labour and Participation. Pour une politique du travail, No. 9 (Paris, ministère du Travail et de la Participation, 1979).

[7] National Assembly: *Rapport*, made by Hélène Missoffe, deputy, on behalf of the Committee on Cultural, Family and Social Affairs on Bill No. 1486 to amend and supplement

the Labour Code's provisions concerning women's work. Appendix to the proceedings of the sitting held on 17 April 1975, No. 1561, p. 11.

[8] "Grossesse et liberté de la femme", in *Droit social* (Paris), Sep.-Oct. 1977, p. 287.

[9] We are thinking of the legislative provisions which emancipated married women in 1975 and, in 1970, shared parental authority between the father and the mother by annulling the exclusive rights hitherto enjoyed by the former.

[10] "Vers une nouvelle condition de la femme au travail", in *Droit social*, Jan. 1976.

[11] Sociology assistant at the University of Nantes. Paper submitted to the Annual Symposium of the French Faculty of Sociology on the theme "Institution familiale et travail des femmes", Nantes, 6-7 June 1980.

[12] See Fichier français des conventions collectives: *Analyse des clauses concernant le travail des femmes parmi les conventions collectives* (Paris, 1978).

[13] Quite recently (4 July 1980), Nicole Pasquier, Secretary of State for Female Employment, asked the Higher Council for the Prevention of Occupational Hazards to consider during the next few months what could be done to soften those provisions of labour law that tend to obstruct women's access to employment, e.g. by relaxing the prohibition on the employment of women in certain trades and in night work, or provisions that do not have widespread application in practice such as the employer's obligation to provide a nursing room. See *Le Figaro* (Paris), 12-13 July 1980.

International Labour Review, Vol. 119, No. 6, November-December 1980

Temporary employment subsidies in industrialised market economies

C. J. AISLABIE *

1. Introduction

Over the past decade the industrialised market economies have experienced rising unemployment levels and a declining confidence in the efficacy of demand-management measures. This has led to calls for governments to take steps which have an immediate effect on levels of employment in the private sector. At the same time governments are also being urged to pursue industrial, regional and structural adjustment policies to ensure that the right kind of jobs are available in the medium term.[1] However, there are differences of opinion as to the relationship between short-term[2] and medium-term measures. To some, short-term measures are needed until those with medium-term outcomes make themselves felt,[3] while to others these short-term measures are expedients, possibly counter-productive in their effects,[4] which encourage ad hoc[5] interventions in the economy. There is also a school of thought which treats the distinctions drawn immediately above as illusory, reasoning that industrial, regional and structural adjustment policies have themselves become, as a result of the pressure of rising unemployment levels, short-term expedients.

The discussion raises a number of issues as to the status of short-term measures to relieve unemployment. Firstly, there is the definitional problem. We do not want to have to consider every measure which is said to have a short-term influence on employment levels. Secondly, assuming that the government has determined upon some microeconomic intervention in the economy, the question arises whether short-term measures are necessarily inferior to their medium-term counterparts. Finally, attention has to be paid to the role of these short-term measures in the light of the other available instruments of economic policy.

In this article we shall first explain the concept of temporary employment subsidies (TES), paying particular attention to the reasons

* Senior Lecturer in Economics, University of Newcastle, New South Wales, Australia.

why they should be distinguished from an industrial, regional or structural adjustment policy. Secondly, we examine the three main classes of subsidy: those concerned with job retention, those concerned with job creation and those concerned with providing investment inducements. Thirdly, possible limitations of TES are discussed and this is followed by a section which examines the rationales advanced for their use. Finally, it is suggested that a clarification of the role of TES will make them more effective and place the criticisms which have been levelled against them in better perspective.

2. Forms of assistance to industry

State aids: a taxonomy

To understand what is meant by TES it is necessary to know something of the different forms of assistance provided by government to industry in industrialised market economies.

To begin with, we are not concerned with all governmental involvement in industry, only with what has been termed an intervention. What is meant by an intervention is captured by Article 92(1)[6] of the Treaty of Rome establishing the European Economic Community. It involves four elements: government funding, an interference with market forces, a preference for certain enterprises[7] and an impact on international trade.[8] The intervention is usually on the supply side through, in effect, the provision of subsidised inputs, although interventions on the demand side or directly affecting the profitability of the enterprise have also occurred.[9]

It is also useful to make a distinction between a "general aid scheme",[10] which is potentially available to all enterprises without discrimination, and aid schemes which only apply to a restricted range of enterprises through being, for example, sectorally or regionally specific. The latter are termed "selective interventions".

To complete our taxonomy it is necessary to note that both general aid schemes and selective interventions can be classified according to the principal goal being pursued, such as full employment, a healthy balance of payments, low rates of inflation or distributional equity. Furthermore, within each such classification a distinction can be made between short-term measures on the one hand and medium-term measures on the other.

State aids for temporary employment purposes

TES are state aids whose principal purpose is to reduce the level of unemployment. It is true that many selective interventions in industry offer, as an apparent side-benefit, increased employment and it is certainly claimed that these are, in effect, employment subsidy schemes of either a temporary or a permanent nature. This is an issue which we shall take up in the next section, where we shall also consider whether these schemes are likely to last for longer than a limited period of time.

It is useful to note that TES can be either selective interventions or general aid schemes. This fact has been the source of some confusion and possibly misinformed comment. As we shall see below, the differing economic rationales advanced for these schemes would imply recourse to selective interventions in some cases and to general aid schemes in others.

Other state aids

During a period of rising unemployment it may at first sight appear to be difficult to identify forms of assistance which are principally concerned with alleviating unemployment. This is because emphasis is likely to be placed on the employment implications of almost any form of assistance to industry. Nevertheless, a distinction can be drawn between cases where the primary object of providing the assistance is to reduce unemployment and cases where some other concern predominates. Where it is difficult to draw such a distinction a test which can be applied is to consider what the government would do if, for some reason, it could not proceed with the assistance in question. If, as a last resort, it would be willing to provide a quite different form of assistance in order to be able to achieve the same anticipated impact on unemployment, then there can be little doubt that the state aid in question is an employment measure.

In practice it may be much easier than the above suggests to distinguish employment subsidy schemes from state aids provided as part of industrial, regional, structural adjustment and similar policies. This is because the former seek to make an immediate impact while the whole thrust of the latter is towards effecting more enduring changes in the economy. This is not to suggest that government programmes in support of the former may not extend over a considerable number of years or that programmes in support of the latter will necessary last longer than the time between one budget and another. It should be noted that, in some cases, governments accept the fact that subsidising employment will only provide jobs for a limited period of time while, in others, there is an expectation (or at least a hope) that even when the subsidy is withdrawn workers will be able to keep their jobs or find new ones thanks to the training and experience gained during the period of subsidisation. Even in this latter case, however, the employment subsidy should be regarded as a temporary measure.

3. The main purposes served by TES

It is possible to distinguish three broad approaches to the development of TES. A firm may be encouraged to retain workers it might otherwise have declared redundant, it may be given an incentive to provide employment (albeit of a temporary nature) to the unemployed (and particularly to those lacking adequate work experience) or it may be provided with an inducement to invest (in plant and machinery, or even in inventories, better methods and new products). Each of these approaches will be discussed in turn below with the aid of appropriate examples.

Employment retention

While it is very tempting to visualise the unemployment problem as one of preventing redundancies (and the elimination of positions previously held by those who resign or retire), it is better understood as relating to the inability of those who seek it to find gainful employment. Rising unemployment levels can be consistent with stable and even rising levels of employment when the proportion of the population seeking employment increases. In these circumstances the elimination of unemployment may require more positive measures than an elimination of redundancies. It may be that the road to full employment will entail more rather than less structural adjustment in the economy. But, even putting dynamic considerations to one side, TES can raise some awkward problems in a static framework.

From a static point of view the employment subsidy appears at first sight to offer lower unemployment for a moderate budgetary outlay. The difficulty lies in devising practicable methods of administering a scheme so that the government is not offering a larger inducement than necessary, is not subsidising employment in some firms at the expense of jobs elsewhere and is not paying for workers declared redundant simply in order to obtain the subsidy.[11] The significance of these problems is a matter for conjecture[12] but there can be little doubt that their existence encourages variability in scheme design as governments strive to obtain the maximum reduction in unemployment levels for a given budgetary outlay.

The United Kingdom scheme provides an example of a subsidy which is available without the restrictions on eligibility to be found in some schemes.[13] With a nil displacement effect,[14] the flat-rate subsidy of £20 per week would lower unemployment and provide the Government with two valuable offsets: assuming average earnings of £45 per week, a reduction in expenditure on unemployment-related benefits in the region of £16 per week plus, on the income side, approximately £17 per week in additional income tax and social security contributions. The actual cost to the Government can only be a subject for speculation but the budgetary outlays amounted to £275 million between August 1975 and March 1978, at which time 180,000 workers were being subsidised each week. It should be noted that this subsidy is only granted for three months at a time but that any firm can enjoy extensions up to 18 months.

A number of variants on this basic strategy of giving the firm a subsidy to avert redundancies can now be briefly considered. Firstly, it is possible to defer redundancies to a more favourable time of the year from the point of view of employment prospects. The National Labour Market Board (AMS) of Sweden has placed public orders with industry in order to postpone local shutdowns of industrial plants from winter to the spring or summer.[15] Secondly, it may be possible to ensure that employees receive adequate notice of termination of employment. The AMS can support a bankrupt firm for up to six months with this end in view.[16] Thirdly, the subsidy can be confined to workers expected to have particular difficulty in finding new employment. Among the measures taken to support the Swedish textile and clothing industries is a subsidy of 15 kronor[17] per hour for employees over 50 years of age, who form one-third of the workforce in these industries.[18] Fourthly, the subsidy can be made conditional upon the provision by firms of training to their employees: Swedish firms in financial difficulties can receive a subsidy of 25 kronor per hour for each participating employee up to a maximum of 960 hours per person.[19]

The interesting common feature in most of these examples is that they minimise the displacement effect and the danger that redundancies will be declared solely in order to obtain the subsidy. However, these schemes have not grappled with the problem of obtaining the highest possible employment retention for a given budgetary allocation by reducing subsidy payments to those firms which, had they been given a smaller subsidy, would have retained all or part of the workforce declared to need subsidisation.

Job creation

Two basic policy options are available in job creation. The emphasis can be placed on the recruitment of employees in nominated categories or on raising the firm's total level of employment.

Because of the "catch-22" situation faced by many of the unemployed, and particularly the young unemployed, i.e. the fact that they are frequently not considered for the available vacancies because they lack the experience and training which they might have gained had they been employed, there exists a wide variety of TES which seek to overcome this obvious barrier to employability. Nevertheless, the widespread interest taken in them[20] should not blind us to the fact that they, like most job creation schemes, experience much the same administrative problems as employment retention schemes. This helps to explain the variety of arrangements to be found in practice. The most obvious difficulty is confining the subsidy to those who really need it. Indeed, even if the subsidised employer does not recruit the trained and experienced, he is tempted to take on employees whose other qualifications make them employable or who only just fail to meet his usual standards. This is not to argue that the unskilled and the semi-skilled are unemployable but simply that they form a group which is very vulnerable to recession, very difficult to help through selective employment programmes[21] and, as a group, most likely to need a general expansion of the economy as a prerequisite for improved employment prospects.

Most of the employees recruited in nominated categories are usually young although it has not been unknown for schemes of this sort to cater for, or be extended to, other workers who have special difficulty in obtaining employment. For example, there was the United States' Job Opportunities in the Business Sector (JOBS). Its objective was to encourage the employment of members of disadvantaged groups who needed on-the-job training and support services in jobs requiring a significant level of skill.[22] Here, however, although the target of 500,000 jobs within three years starting in mid-1968 was almost met, the retention rate was only 47 per cent.[23]

More recent schemes can be divided into those which also involve on-the-job training and those which do not. All these schemes usually have age limits, requirements relating to minimum periods of employment and other eligibility conditions pertaining to the employee and, sometimes, the firm.[24] In some cases, for example in Norway and Sweden, schemes involving training run side-by-side with those which do not.[25] Almost all schemes have rules which insist that the new recruit be under 25 years of age[26] although lower maximum ages are quite common.[27] Several schemes seek to cater for apprentices whose training is in danger of being interrupted.[28]

The remaining job creation schemes to consider are those which place no restriction on the employee who may be recruited except that he or she may have had to be unemployed for some stated period of time before becoming eligible for assistance. The firm has to satisfy eligibility conditions which usually are designed to ensure that its total level of employment increases, even if only for a specific length of time.[29] Most countries[30] which have an unrestricted scheme also have one where the subsidy is limited to the recruitment of employees in nominated categories.[31]

Investment inducements

Most of the TES considered so far have an impact on aggregate employment because lower real wage costs for marginal employees induce an increased use of the labour factor. In the case of some other TES an induced increase in output necessitates a greater employment of factors but no change in factor proportions.

Undoubtedly the best known among the latter group of TES is that which operates in Sweden to allow tax relief on profits which are placed in an account with the Central Bank. These can only be drawn upon for investment purposes in accordance with prescribed rules.[32] Other methods of encouraging investments which serve as cyclical equalisers are to bring forward planned projects in the public sector,[33] or the use of inducements in the private sector.[34]

Valuable as these incentives to investment may be, they only have a limited impact on the available spare capacity in the economy. However, in a Swedish scheme, inventory levels are subsidised in order to encourage the maintenance of employment levels.[35] It is interesting to note in this regard that when the British machine tool industry sought a stockpiling assistance scheme the Department of Industry preferred to help it to modernise and develop new tools.[36]

Finally, mention should be made of structural or trade adjustment assistance, which inhabits a borderland between industrial policy and temporary employment policy. Whereas industrial policy is more usually regarded as involving product diversification, this form of assistance more often than not encourages process differentiation. This enables the firm to compete more effectively in its own industry rather than transfer its resources elsewhere. Furthermore, the aid, whatever its ostensible rationale, can be both a compensation for adverse government decisions (e.g. a reduction in the level of protection) and a form of temporary assistance to allow time for adjusting to changed circumstances.[37]

4. Possible limitations of TES

Effectiveness in general

TES have been strongly criticised on the grounds of limited effectiveness. It is argued by some that no acceptable analysis of the unemployment problem would suggest that it could be solved by creating temporary jobs, and by others that TES divert funds away from measures which would ensure higher levels of employment in the medium term.

As far as the first of these arguments is concerned, the rationales advanced in support of TES will be examined in more detail below. However, it can be noted in passing that there would appear to be quite strong evidence that much unemployment in industrialised market economies is of a temporary nature. There are plausible reasons for believing that the recession will end, even if it cannot be predicted when this will occur, and that, in the subsequent economic expansion, the level of unemployment will be substantially reduced. Similarly, experience suggests that, given sufficient time, serious pools of unemployment do tend to dry up. Furthermore, although TES are short-term in nature, subsidies can be given right through an extended period of recession. Consequently, it is difficult not to believe that TES make some contribution to reducing unemployment. Of course, this is not to claim that TES deal with the underlying causes of unemployment or that only TES should be used to "cure" or alleviate unemployment.

Turning to the diversion of funds argument, this may be expressed in terms which stress the folly of undertaking palliative measures within the present economic structures or in terms which stress the areas in which it is claimed the funds would be better spent. The first approach is based on the contention that unemployment has its source in changes in the economy (such as advances in technology) which mean that consumers are never likely to buy as much as some industries are capable of producing. The difficulty with this contention is that while changes of this kind do occur and do contribute to unemployment problems, there is no way of proving that market economies will not be able to surmount these problems in the future as they have in the past. Furthermore, while there may be some truth in this claim in respect to some industries, even in its most extreme form it does not imply that most industries will not offer much the same kind of employment opportunity as they always have when the recession does come to an end.

The second approach to the diversion of funds argument places stress on the need to give priority to measures with a medium- to long-term effect undertaken as part of a, say, growth, industrial or regional policy. Now, while it is undeniable that funds spent with some temporary purpose in view frequently do not achieve any lasting effect, such an argument is only decisive if it can be demonstrated that the government cannot better attain some policy goal through the use of a temporary measure or that by some quirk of the budgetary process the allocation of funds does not reflect the government's real priorities. It is not possible to accept that one or both of these conditions generally hold. Consequently, TES cannot be ruled out on these grounds.

The discussion suggests that TES should not be discarded on the grounds of limited over-all effectiveness. The arguments advanced to discredit them involve claims that there is more to an understanding of the unemployment problem than is usually taken into account in devising TES. However, there is nothing in the thinking underlying TES which precludes government action being directed against other aspects of the unemployment problem.

Effectiveness in attaining stated objectives

The above claims that TES are ineffective were couched in very general terms. Politicians and administrators are far more interested in evaluations of the ability of TES to achieve their stated objectives.

The first of the principal stated objectives is to even out the business cycle. This objective has its roots in contemporary thinking which does not accept that the alternating phases of expansion and contraction in the economy are beyond government control. We should note here that there is an inconsistency in a government placing faith in the employment-generating powers of the additional funds expended on TES if it has no confidence in higher levels of government expenditure as a general cure for unemployment. Nevertheless, the effect of reducing unemployment during a recession may be obtained from TES even though the government is not able to find a budget formula which allows it to achieve its over-all employment (and other economic) goals.

The second objective is to minimise the budgetary cost of unemployment by reducing the total outlay on unemployment benefits. Now, whether TES do this depends on the precise nature of each scheme. In particular, the extent to which the scheme reduces unemployment by eliminating employment prospects elsewhere in the economy is crucial in determining the real cost of these schemes. It can be noted, in passing, that more might be done in the way of sharing the available work more evenly. However, there appears to be little doubt that TES can be devised which, if they can be made to function as they are expected to, should reduce the budgetary cost of unemployment.

The third main objective is to reduce the total number of unemployed by providing work for, or protecting the jobs of, persons who satisfy particular criteria. This has its origin in contemporary manpower policy with its concern about "mismatches" between the skills and experience of the unemployed and those likely to be required by employers with vacancies to fill. This objective would appear to be the one which dominates current thinking on the question of employment subsidies. However, a considerable variety of opinion exists as to which of the unemployed should benefit. In some cases this reflects a desire to achieve the greatest possible reduction in unemployment for a given expenditure level by making the subsidy scheme as attractive as possible to the employer. In other cases the government is assumed to have a better knowledge of the longer-term needs of industry than is to be obtained from current market signals or to be working on the assumption that the most disadvantaged need the most assistance. It is unfortunate that, while TES seek to reduce aggregate unemployment by reducing unemployment in particular areas, there is no clear understanding of the relationship between attempts to reduce unemployment in these areas and their effects on aggregate unemployment. But it is likely that this problem does more to restrict the wide use of TES than to affect the workings of particular TES.

Side-effects

Besides criticisms of TES which cast doubts on their effectiveness, there are others which suggest that they can have adverse side-effects. In particular, it is claimed that TES are detrimental to the process whereby countries specialise in producing those goods in whose production they have some inherent advantage and to the process whereby economies adjust to allow this specialisation in production. These points will be examined in turn.

Government assistance to industry which affects its international competitiveness can be divided into two categories. The assistance can be provided as part of a process whose ultimate aim is to ensure that domestic industry specialises in producing those goods in which it has some inherent advantage. Alternatively, it may be given in accordance with a policy which seeks to ensure that all, or part, of particular domestic markets are reserved for domestic producers even though this intention may not be frankly acknowledged. Where the assistance falls into the first category it is difficult not to accept assurances that the most expedient path to a more efficient allocation of resources is being taken.

It may be objected that, whatever the intentions may be, subsidies are unlikely to be removed until the economy has actually adjusted so that the domestic industry can compete once more on international markets. If this is so, they are suspect because they provide, if not an incentive not to adjust, at least some compensation for not having done so. This argument would be more plausible if most TES were, in practice, selective interventions. However, since most are general aids it would appear more reasonable to argue that the continued existence of TES is likely to be encouraged at least as much by the persistence of unacceptable levels of unemployment as by the problems facing particular industries.

While TES in some cases may be associated with a protective attitude towards domestic industry, it is more likely that their protective use reflects a desire to insulate domestic industry from international market forces than that the schemes themselves encourage protective attitudes. Eliminating TES would only change the garb with which protective impulses are clothed.

A new policy instrument

Most of the arguments advanced to support the claim that TES are ineffective have been shown to be based on an inadequate appreciation of what governments are seeking to do with these schemes. It is true that TES are not based on any profound analysis of the sources of, and possible remedies for, unemployment. This is because, paradoxical though it may seem, TES have *not* been dedicated to the goal of eliminating unemployment. Such schemes depend for their usefulness on the assumption that governments need a policy instrument which allows them, by producing some immediate alleviation of the problem, to "buy time" during which other policy instruments and/or the market mechanism will reduce unemployment to more acceptable levels. In particular, governments are reluctant to consider medium-term solutions to a problem which may be transitory, to abandon mildly deflationary policies which are believed, rightly or wrongly, to have at least a short-term adverse effect on employment, and to retreat from a commitment to international specialisation in production which is considered to provide a significant boost to growth and to demand for labour in the medium term.

This interpretation of TES is not accepted by those who point to the wide variety of TES, the evidence that they are sometimes introduced hastily as political palliatives, and the retarding effect they can have on structural adjustment in industry. But any argument that governments react to higher levels of unemployment by arbitrarily guaranteeing long-term job security in some cases and not in others must fail as a general proposition not because they have never done so but because so much of the relevant intervention in industry is short-term in character and consistent with expectations that certain kinds of short-term measures are likely to be efficacious in practice.

5. Economic rationales for the use of TES

Most discussions of TES have centred more on the technicalities of devising effective measures than on exploring fundamental questions relating to the causes of, and cures for, unemployment. These discussions tend to imply that TES should function satisfactorily provided adequate administrative procedures can be developed.

Cyclical equalisation

The cyclical equalisation rationale is based on an assumption as to the nature of the economic environment in which TES will operate. In this rationale stress is laid on the likelihood that any period of recession is merely an interlude before the economy begins expanding again. Consequently, social, if not private, benefits can be gained by bringing forward investment, production and training into the recession period so as to reduce pressures on the economy during the upswing. Since, in general, it presumably does not matter whereabouts in the economy cyclical equalisation occurs, this rationale encourages the use of TES as general aid schemes.

While this rationale appears to be little more than a particular application of the general proposition that governments should seek to control the level of aggregate demand at all stages of the business cycle in order to damp down fluctuations in aggregate employment, TES can be regarded as institutional arrangements whereby governments seek to offset the deflationary forces at work in the economy in such a way that any increase in government expenditure is concentrated on giving an immediate stimulus to employment. In recent years the need for TES has become more apparent as, in many industrialised market economies, periods of sustained expansion, particularly periods coupled with dramatic declines in the number of those unemployed, have become less frequent.[38] This change in economic circumstances has led to changes in expectations which have effects on both the supply and the demand side of markets. For example, there is some evidence that both employers and employees are increasingly reluctant to train and be trained solely or primarily at their own expense.

Labour immobility

The cyclical equalisation rationale for TES was developed at a time when it was assumed that governments could effectively control the level of economic aggregates such as employment, demand and investment. While a decline in confidence in this ability does not diminish the value of the contribution TES can make to cyclical equalisation, it does lead to TES being also seen as part of the answer to that part of the unemployment problem which reflects a malfunction of the economy in some "structural" sense. Attention has been focused on the general slowness with which labour resources respond to changes in market signals, and this has been advanced as a major reason why governments should seek to intervene on a temporary basis in the private sector. In particular, it is argued that labour markets function imperfectly, imposing costs on those looking for employment. Consequently, it is considered desirable to allow those facing redundancy as much time as possible to obtain a new post before they lose their old job. This is regarded as being particularly important in cases where a large number of employees are likely to be made redundant at the same time. It should be noted that although this rationale should, and to some extent does, encourage the design of TES as selective interventions, many TES which appear to be more readily explicable in terms of this rationale are designed as general aid schemes. This results from a desire to assist as many of the unemployed as possible, thus forcing an emphasis on administrative simplicity in scheme design.

Cost-benefit analysis

Both the rationales considered so far assume that TES will yield a worth-while reduction in unemployment in return for the funds expended. In the cost-benefit analysis rationale it is argued that many TES will be justifiable if costs are compared with benefits (even if this is done in rather informal terms). This rationale comes in one of two forms. Either it is argued that there will be no net cost to the government from a properly administered scheme or it is argued that there will be no net social cost once all the costs imposed on society by unemployment are taken into account. But, as we saw in the case of the British TES scheme discussed above,[39] calculations of this nature tend to be heavily dependent on an assumption that the scheme operates in an "ideal" way, for example that there is no displacement effect. Once the cost of the subsidy increases, the government will be interested not only in determining whether the benefits outweigh the costs but also in the different cost-benefit ratios characterising alternative approaches to reducing unemployment, with possibly lower costs of subsidy per additional person employed. It should be noted that this also is a rationale which might well encourage the design of TES as selective interventions. However, given the informality of most approaches to cost-benefit analysis in this area, there is a considerable willingness to believe that most schemes would pass the cost-benefit test and, consequently, that net benefits are maximised by extending the subsidies to as many of the unemployed as can be plausibly included in one scheme or another.

Comparative cost disadvantage

The final rationale, which is more controversial than the three discussed above, holds that subsidies can lead to an increase in aggregate employment by partly offsetting the immediate comparative cost disadvantages affecting many industries that are shedding labour.

The objections made to this rationale are that subsidies which seek to increase employment at the expense of a trading partner abroad invite retaliation in the form of comparative programmes of subsidisation, discourage the process of structural adjustment in industry and are a poor substitute for a devaluation should domestic and foreign cost levels be seriously out of alignment. While admitting the force of these arguments, there may well be a case for using TES for a limited period in a small number of industries which cannot be effectively assisted in other ways (provided competitive subsidisation is unlikely or is controlled by international agreement) in order to "buy time" to allow an industry and its employees to adjust to changed circumstances. Once again it may be noted that the rationale tends to suggest that TES should be selective interventions even though the element of selectivity in TES design may be missing in practice.

6. Improving the efficacy of TES

The role of TES

While the discussion of the rationales for the use of TES may suggest that circumstances exist in which these subsidies have something to contribute, none of the rationales considered can be said to provide a convincing explanation of the role TES are expected to play in the relief of unemployment. One reason for this must surely be that, with declining confidence in the efficacy of demand-management methods, governments in industrialised market economy countries are losing faith in their ability to reach their immediate employment and other major economic goals such as stable prices, high levels of economic growth and a healthy balance of payments. Reduced unemployment is increasingly seen as a goal which will be attained only after other economic goals have been reached.

The existence of TES does not necessarily contradict this point of view. An examination of the case for subsidies in the previous section indicates that the role of TES in reducing unemployment is unclear. Cyclical equalisation emerges as only part of a programme of counter-cyclical expenditures, the labour immobility argument is frequently thought to be equally applicable to the medium and to the short term and a cost-benefit approach is concerned with reducing government expenditure as much as with reducing unemployment. And, whatever else might be said about the comparative cost disadvantage rationale, it is very doubtful whether current levels of unemployment in the industrialised market economies arise primarily from any loss of competitive advantage in international trade.

Our discussion has also suggested that the implementation of TES reflects a misunderstanding of the most appropriate role for these subsidies. Unless TES are to be seen solely as cyclical equalisation measures, they are only likely to be effective when used selectively in the most appropriate circumstances. Despite this, many TES are clearly conceived as if the coverage of particular schemes (rather than the number of well designed schemes) should be one of the principal criteria by which the TES contribution to reducing unemployment should be judged.

Developing a satisfactory role for TES will involve a re-examination of government expenditure priorities at various stages of the business cycle. Even if we must accept that a tight rein has to be kept on aggregate levels of government expenditure, this does not preclude the development of more flexible policies towards the composition of this expenditure. Three things in particular need to be done. Firstly, labour-intensive expenditures need to be reserved as far as possible for periods of recession. Secondly, TES need to be funded in ways which allow the level of funding to vary directly with the level of unemployment. This allows the labour supply to respond more readily to pressures for structural adjustment during periods of expansion. Finally, the on-going obligations incurred by all government expenditure programmes need to be carefully monitored, particularly during expansionary phases when controls over public expenditure tend to be relaxed.

In an ideal world the composition of government expenditures would vary in labour intensity over the business cycle. In practice, governments have to take specific steps to encourage labour-intensive expenditures during periods of recession and this provides a role for TES in economic policy. Since it is unlikely that the labour intensity of government expenditures in each industry at a particular point in time can be identical, it is to be expected that TES will take the form of selective (labour-intensive) interventions rather than general aids.

Overcoming the suggested TES limitations

We did not accept above that any of the criticisms levelled at TES demonstrated that they suffered from major shortcomings or justified refusing to use them. Nevertheless, it is interesting to look again at the suggested limitations of TES because, having clarified the role played by these subsidies, it is possible to see the criticisms in better perspective.

Clarifying the role of TES is important because unless we identify their expected contribution to economic policy-making it is impossible to determine criteria by which they may be judged. Where these subsidies are represented as being not only an "answer" to unemployment but one which might even reduce government expenditure, it is only to be expected that TES will tend to be judged in the light of such exaggerated claims. Once a meaningful role has been established for TES attention is focused on the real question at issue. This is whether TES, implemented as part of some anti-unemployment policy, can realistically be expected to make a significant contribution to the furtherance of that policy.

Accepting that TES have a role to play in reducing unemployment blunts the diversion of funds argument. The case for government funding of medium-term measures is different from that for short-term measures and each has to be argued on its merits. By the same token, although TES might be used for various other stated objectives of government policy and, consequently, must be judged in relation to the relevant objective, we would prefer to focus attention on one which makes most sense within the broad framework of economic policy.

Specifying a role for TES does not preclude these subsidies from exercising a protective influence vis-à-vis domestic industry. However, it does identify the stages of the business cycle during which structural adjustment measures should be concentrated. Finally, it can be noted that the proposed role for TES places more emphasis on the contribution these subsidies can make to reducing unemployment and less emphasis on their "buying time" aspects which have tended to dominate contemporary official thinking.

A specific proposal

The main conclusion of this paper is clearly that TES represent an important new development but that they have met with a very mixed response because of the lack of a persuasive rationale for their use. The clarification of the role of TES will be pervasive in its effect and little is gained by trying to speculate on the various ways in which it might have some impact on these schemes except to suggest that, in the short term at least, a reappraisal of the rationale(s) underlying present TES might lead to their modification or abandonment. We would expect this to happen because it is possible that a re-evaluation of the contribution some TES are making would raise doubts as to whether they are actually reducing unemployment at all. These doubts would tend to be encouraged by a realisation that what was intended as a selective intervention in the economy has often become a general aid likely to be used both in areas where it may be effective and in areas where its effectiveness is less certain.

The taxonomy of state aids developed above is more than just an explanatory device since it has implications for the type and resource demands of the administrative processes necessary to implement them successfully. In broad terms a general aid seeks to obtain the advantages which flow from administrative simplicity and a neutral effect (as between different sectors of the economy) at the risk of influencing the incentive structure in areas to which the economic intervention in question was not deliberately directed. By the same token, a selective intervention may well have the implied advantages—and disadvantages—of not being a general aid. On balance, we would consider the ability to devise more specific instruments of economic policy and to confine intervention to those areas of the economy which are policy-relevant would outweigh any losses arising from administrative costs and departures from a more efficient pattern of resource allocation. But to make selective interventions truly selective, governments need to establish a sufficiently detailed planning machinery to enable them to discriminate, on the basis of a close knowledge of the particular employment markets and industrial technology, between cases where TES can significantly reduce unemployment and cases where they would affect the composition but not the level of unemployment.

Notes

[1] Approximately, from two to five years.

[2] Up to about two years.

[3] Or until the economy picks up of its own accord or as a direct result of demand-management techniques.

[4] By imposing costs on other firms, by discouraging structural adjustment at the firm level and by competing for the limited funds available for microeconomic interventions.

[5] Ad hoc, in this context, can be taken to imply either that all selective interventions (or even all microeconomic interventions) in the economy are wrong or that such interventions should only be undertaken in order to produce specific desired medium-term effects.

[6] "... any aid granted by a Member State or through state resources, in any form whatsoever, which distorts or threatens to distort competition by favouring certain enterprises or the production of certain goods shall, to the extent to which it affects trade between Member States, be incompatible with the common market".

[7] Or, as the Article cited in note 6 adds, "the production of certain goods".

[8] For further discussion of what state aids mean in the EEC context see G. Schrans: "National and regional aid to industry under the EEC Treaty", in *Common Market Law Review* (Alphen aan den Rijn), May 1973, pp. 175-181.

[9] For a list of measures considered state aids in the EEC context see A. Dashwood and T. Sharpe: "The Industry Acts 1972 and 1975 and European Community Law: Part 1", ibid., Feb. 1978, p. 12.

[10] Defined by Dashwood and Sharpe (loc. cit.) as "a scheme whereby state assistance is granted to undertakings in whatever business or location for purposes which are typically ill-defined but which are normally expressed in terms of encouraging economic growth or modernisation of the national economy or some such broad formula".

[11] For a discussion of these points see OECD: *A medium term strategy for employment and manpower policies* (Paris, 1978), pp. 67-68.

[12] The OECD Secretariat has prepared estimates of the net cost to the British Government of allocating £260 million to its temporary employment subsidy scheme on the basis of 270,000 subsidised workers with assumed average earnings of £45 per week. The subsidy is £20 per week and the net cost would be −£185 million (i.e. a gain to the Government of £185 million) if no unsubsidised workers were displaced but would rise to +£60 million if 60 per cent of the jobs involved represented a displacement of unsubsidised workers. Ibid., p. 69.

[13] Ibid., pp. 68-69.

[14] See note 12.

[15] "Active manpower policy in Sweden", in *Fact Sheets on Sweden* (Stockholm), Oct. 1974, p. 3.

[16] Ibid.

[17] 1 Swedish krona = US$0.23 or £0.11.

[18] Study Group on Structural Adjustment: *Report* (Canberra, Australian Government Publishing Service, 1979), Vol. 2, pp. 11.1.26-27.

[19] B. A. Ericsson: "The employment situation in Sweden: some main issues looking ahead to the 1980s", in *Current Sweden* (Stockholm), May 1979, pp. 4-5.

[20] A particularly valuable reference is OECD: *Youth unemployment* (Paris, 1978), Vol. II.

[21] There are very few industrial plants in the industrialised market economies which have a labour-intensive technology using a high proportion of unskilled and semi-skilled workers. In cases where such an appropriate technology can be found it is difficult to act without adversely affecting the trading opportunities of the less developed countries. For this reason projects to assist young people are more likely to be in the public rather than the private sector. For example, the United Kingdom Job Creation Programme, which provides funds for community-sponsored, labour-intensive, non-profit schemes, seeks to give priority to young people and to emphasise projects which involve environmental improvement and the training needs of young people (OECD: *A medium term strategy*. . ., op. cit., pp. 72-73). This may also partly explain the negative attitude to employment subsidy schemes—whether for youth or others—taken by those who attended an OECD conference on youth unemployment. See idem: *Youth unemployment*, op. cit., Vol. I, pp. 80-81.

[22] For a brief summary of this scheme see Diane Werneke: "Job creation programmes: the United States experience", in *International Labour Review*, July-Aug. 1976, pp. 52-54.

[23] This scheme has been the subject of a number of evaluative studies, for example O. A. Davis et al.: "An empirical study of the NAB-JOBS program", in *Public Policy* (Cambridge (Massachusetts)), Spring 1973, pp. 235-262.

[24] For example, to qualify under the French scheme—which allowed an exceptional exemption from the employer's social security contribution for newly engaged young people under 25 years of age—a firm must not have laid off any personnel for economic reasons during a specified period of time (OECD: *Youth unemployment*, op. cit., Vol. II, p. 58).

[25] Ibid., pp. 116-118 and 128-129.

[26] Although there is a Swedish scheme where the trainee must be *at least* 25 years of age or have had five years' vocational experience. Ibid., p. 129.

[27] The Norwegians experimented with a scheme in 1976 which was confined to those aged under 18. It was dropped (except for districts where difficulty was experienced in using

other measures) because it was feared that it would lead to demands for a subsidy for the engagement of young people in general. Ibid., p. 117.

[28] In Ireland and Northern Ireland. Ibid., pp. 76-77 and 159-160.

[29] In the case of the Small Firms Employment Subsidy in Great Britain the firm has to have employed fewer than 50 persons on a specified date and be located in a Special Development Area. Ibid., pp. 145-146.

[30] For example, Belgium, Ireland, Norway, Sweden and the United Kingdom. Ibid., passim; and Ericsson, op. cit.

[31] An exception is New Zealand (OECD: *Youth unemployment*, op. cit., Vol. II, pp. 103-106).

[32] "Active manpower policy...", op. cit., p. 3.

[33] For example, see Ericsson, op. cit., p. 4; and OECD: *Youth unemployment*, op. cit., Vol. II, p. 74 (for an Irish scheme).

[34] A. B. Philip: *Creating new jobs: a report on long-term job creation in Britain and Sweden* (London, Policy Studies Institute, 1978), p. 3.

[35] Study Group on Structural Adjustment, op. cit., Vol. 2, pp. 11.1.16-17.

[36] Philip, loc. cit. This is one case, at least, where "good" industrial policy was not supplanted by "bad" employment policy.

[37] See Study Group on Structural Adjustment, op. cit., Vol. 2, appendix 11.1 (overseas industry-specific policy); and G. Edgren: "Employment adjustment to trade under conditions of stagnating growth", in *International Labour Review*, May-June 1978, pp. 289-303.

[38] For a discussion see P. McCracken et al.: *Towards full employment and price stability* (Paris, OECD, 1977), pp. 37-99.

[39] See note 12.

International Labour Review, Vol. 119, No. 6, November-December 1980

Unemployment and underemployment in Jamaica, 1972-78[1]

John GAFAR *

It is generally accepted that one of the goals towards which any economic system should strive is full employment, and it is always instructive to consider how close a particular economy comes to achieving it. This paper attempts to do two things: first, to outline the magnitude of unemployment and underemployment in Jamaica—a small, open, export-propelled, dualistic economy—and, secondly, to offer some explanations of the unemployment problem and some policy proposals on how it might be combated.

1. The level of employment and unemployment

Comparable statistics relating to the labour force, employment and unemployment have been compiled since 1972 and are contained in the labour force surveys published by the Department of Statistics, Government of Jamaica. The labour force is defined to include all persons aged 14 and over not attending school full time who, during the survey week, were employed in any form of economic activity for one hour or more, had jobs but were not working or, although they had no jobs, were looking for work or were in a position to accept work. This definition has the advantage of including the "discouraged worker". Persons without jobs or those who worked for less than one hour during the survey week were excluded from the employed category. The unemployed included all persons wanting work, available for work and looking for work. Table 1 summarises the main characteristics of the labour force for the period 1972-78.

The labour force, which is a proxy for the available supply of labour, increased at a rate of 2.9 per cent per annum during this period and averaged about 42 per cent of the total population, while the participation rate was just over 70 per cent.

* Lecturer, Department of Economics, University of the West Indies, Mona, Jamaica.

Table 1. Main characteristics of the labour force, 1972-78[1]

Item	1972	1973	1974	1975	1976	1977	1978	Average annual growth rate (%)
Population ('000)	1 959	1 982	2 013	2 047	2 083	2 101	2 119	1.3
Population aged 14+ ('000)	1 113	1 148	1 181	1 216	1 260	1 286	1 312	2.7
Labour force ('000)	799	803	820	866	896	918	949	2.9
Employed ('000)	617	622	650	685	679	699	702	2.2
Unemployed ('000)	182	181	170	181	217	219	247	5.2
Participation rate (%)	71.8	69.9	69.4	71.2	71.1	71.4	72.3	.
Unemployment rate (%)	22.9	22.5	20.7	20.9	24.2	23.8	26.0	.

[1] Figures are based on the October survey estimates.
Source: Department of Statistics, Jamaica: *The labour force, 1978.*

Total employment, which is a proxy for the demand for labour at the prevailing real wage, increased from 617,000 in 1972 to 702,000 in 1978, a modest growth of 2.2 per cent a year. Unemployment increased over the period from 182,000 to 247,000, a result which suggests that the prevailing levels of economic activity and labour intensity of production were insufficient to absorb the growth in the labour supply. In relative terms unemployment increased from 22.9 per cent in 1972 to 26.0 per cent in 1978, averaging 23 per cent for the whole period, which is probably one of the highest "open" unemployment rates in the Caribbean.

2. Unemployment and underemployment

In most developing countries with a backward agricultural sector there is a high degree of underutilisation of labour arising from seasonal unemployment and underemployment. Unfortunately we are not in a position to examine the level of seasonal unemployment in Jamaica because there are no published statistics. We shall assume that everyone who works less than the statutory work week is underemployed. Under the provisions of the Minimum Wage Act, 1939, the statutory work week was for the first time defined by law in October 1975 as 40 hours, beyond which workers were to be paid premium rates. The national minimum wage was set in 1975 at J$20 for a 40-hour work week;[2] but in the case of household helpers the maximum work week was 44 hours (for a minimum wage of J$22 per week), beyond which overtime rates were payable. Since 1975 the minimum wage has twice been increased, to J$24 in 1977 and to J$26 in 1979.

Table 2. Percentage distribution of employed labour force by number of hours worked during the October survey week, 1973 and 1978

Hours worked	1973			1978		
	Male	Female	Both sexes	Male	Female	Both sexes
Under 9	1.0	1.8	1.3	0.8	2.3	1.4
9 to under 17	2.0	4.1	2.8	2.1	4.3	3.0
17 to under 25	3.2	4.8	3.8	4.6	7.4	5.7
25 to under 33	7.3	10.1	8.4	8.8	14.9	11.2
33 to under 41	22.1	25.0	23.2	35.6	40.5	37.6
41 to under 49	26.9	25.0	26.2	25.1	16.3	21.7
49 and over	33.8	27.3	31.3	19.8	10.7	16.2
Not stated	3.7	1.9	3.0	3.2	3.6	3.2
Total	**100.0**	**100.0**	**100.0**	**100.0**	**100.0**	**100.0**

Source: Computed by the author from *The labour force, 1978*, op. cit.

Statistics on the number of hours worked have been available since 1973 and are presented in table 2 for 1973 and 1978.

Bruton[3] noted that in poor developing countries labour works for excessively long hours, but in the case of Jamaica there has been a decline in the average work week since 1973. This is partly due to the introduction of a national minimum wage (which has adversely affected the demand for household help and casual workers), the decline in investment and export earnings, balance of payments difficulties and a general contraction of the economy. Persons working fewer than 40 hours a week can be viewed as suffering from visible underemployment, and this is closely related to the level of open unemployment and to labour market imperfections. In 1973 the proportion of the employed labour force working fewer than 33 hours per week was 16.3 per cent; by 1978 it had increased to 21.3 per cent (or 15.7 per cent of the labour force). If we add to this 15.7 per cent the 26 per cent open unemployment in 1978, we find that the unemployed and underemployed together represented approximately 42 per cent of the labour force.

Closely related to the problem of unemployment and underemployment is the distribution of income and its influence on the level of poverty. Bruton suggests that an estimate of the size of the invisibly underemployed labour force can be obtained from an examination of the distribution of income. Those with incomes below a certain level can, for all practical purposes, be defined as invisibly underemployed, since anyone earning less than that amount cannot survive without additional financial resources. It must be emphasised that the income approach presupposes a poverty line or some other measure of poverty and, as Squire[4] has observed, it is analytically very different from the hours-worked approach,

Table 3. Percentage distribution of employed labour force by income group and sex, 1973 and 1978[1]

Income group (average per week)	1973			1978		
	Male	Female	Both sexes	Male	Female	Both sexes
No income	5.8	6.4	6.0	5.5	11.7	8.1
Under J$10	32.8	42.7	36.6	11.1	11.6	11.3
J$10 to under J$20	28.5	29.4	28.9	16.7	16.4	16.5
J$20 to under J$30	13.7	8.9	11.8	15.3	23.3	18.6
J$30 to under J$40	7.8	5.2	6.8	12.2	11.9	12.1
J$40 to under J$50	4.2	2.7	3.6	10.3	6.1	8.6
J$50 to under J$100	5.0	4.1	4.7	20.2	13.3	17.3
J$100 and over	2.2	0.6	1.6	8.7	5.7	7.5
Total	**100.0**	**100.0**	**100.0**	**100.0**	**100.0**	**100.0**

[1] Figures are based on the October survey estimates.
Source: Calculated by the author from *The labour force, 1975* and *1978.*

which is related to the functioning of the labour market. Table 3 presents estimates of the distribution of income for the employed labour force for 1973 and 1978.

The picture is one of unequal distribution. The data suggest that in 1978 at least 40 per cent of the employed labour force (or 29 per cent of the total labour force) was earning less than the national minimum wage of J$24 per week. Add to this 29 per cent invisible underemployment the 26 per cent open unemployment in 1978 and we find that around 55 per cent of the labour force was unemployed or underemployed.

The disparity in the results given by the hours-worked approach and the income approach may arise because the definition of the employed used in labour force statistics includes (i) not only those working for wages but also those working for tips or payment in kind; (ii) trainees not receiving payment; and (iii) persons who spend time in the operation of a business or profession, even though no sales are made or services rendered. In Jamaica the existence of a great number of street vendors (higglers) who sit by the side of the street for hours at a time waiting to sell a few of their wares goes some way towards explaining the difference in the underemployment estimates based on the income and the hours-worked approaches.

Harris[5] has estimated that in 1973 a weekly minimum wage of J$20 was just sufficient to purchase bare essentials. Between October 1973 and October 1978 the inflation rate was such that an average income of at least J$50 per week would have been needed in 1978 in order to sustain the 1973 purchasing value of J$20. On this basis, the data in table 3 indicate that approximately three-quarters of the employed labour force in 1978 (or

Table 4. Labour force characteristics by sex, 1972-78

Item	1972	1973	1974	1975	1976	1977	1978	Average annual rate of growth (%)
Male								
Population ('000)	957	951	974	992	1 017	1 028	1 042	1.4
Population aged 14+ ('000)	529	540	558	576	607	614	629	2.9
Labour force ('000)	445	445	455	470	489	494	504	2.1
Employed ('000)	381	385	397	414	417	422	425	1.8
Unemployed ('000)	64	60	58	56	72	72	79	3.6
Participation rate (%)	84.1	82.4	81.5	81.6	80.6	80.5	80.1	.
Unemployment rate (%)	14.5	13.4	12.7	11.9	14.7	14.6	15.7	.
Female								
Population ('000)	1 002	1 031	1 039	1 055	1 066	1 073	1 077	1.2
Population aged 14+ ('000)	584	608	623	640	653	672	683	2.6
Labour force ('000)	354	358	365	396	407	424	445	3.9
Employed ('000)	236	237	253	271	262	277	277	2.7
Unemployed ('000)	118	121	112	125	145	147	168	6.1
Participation rate (%)	60.6	58.9	58.6	61.9	62.3	63.1	65.2	.
Unemployment rate (%)	33.4	33.8	30.6	31.7	35.6	34.7	37.7	.

Source: *The labour force, 1978*, op. cit.

some 55 per cent of the total labour force) were underemployed, and if we add to this the 26 per cent of open unemployment we find that over 80 per cent of the labour force was below the poverty line.

3. Employment and unemployment by sex

It has frequently been observed that female unemployment tends to be higher than male unemployment because, for historical, cultural or other reasons, it has become accepted that it is primarily the responsibility of the man to provide for his family. The breakdown of the level of employment, unemployment and certain other key labour force features by sex is summarised in table 4.

The statistics show that the male labour force increased by more than 13 per cent between 1972 and 1978, compared with an increase of 25.7 per cent for females. The increase in the female labour force arises from the state of the economy, which has compelled women to seek work, and from

Table 5. Percentage distribution of the unemployed labour force by age and sex, 1972 and 1978[1]

Age group	1972			1978		
	Male	Female	Both sexes	Male	Female	Both sexes
14-19	56.9	42.2	47.2	37.2	25.2	29.1
20-24				23.0	26.1	25.1
25-34	18.0	25.3	22.8	18.9	21.0	20.3
35-44	10.5	16.6	14.5	8.8	12.1	11.0
45-54	6.0	8.7	7.8	5.1	8.3	7.2
55-64	6.1	5.7	5.8	5.1	5.0	5.0
65 and over	2.5	1.5	1.9	1.9	2.3	2.2
Total	**100.0**	**100.0**	**100.0**	**100.0**	**100.0**	**100.0**

[1] October survey estimates.
Source: *The labour force, 1972* and *1978.*

the increased opportunities for female employment provided by the authorities under the Special Employment Programme (e.g. public works and street cleaning). The average participation rate for males is about 80 per cent compared with 60 for females. Male employment accounted for nearly 61 per cent of the total, while the average unemployment rates for males and females over the period were about 14 and 34 per cent respectively.

4. Unemployment by age and sex

Table 5 presents figures on the distribution of unemployment by age and sex for the years 1972 and 1978. It reveals a heavy preponderance of unemployment in the age group 14-24, which accounted for approximately one-half of the total unemployed labour force. In a study on the level of unemployment in Trinidad and Tobago, Farrell[6] observed that about 60 per cent of the unemployed are between the ages of 15 and 24. In most countries unemployment among the young tends to be higher than among older persons because the young usually have less job experience and less knowledge of the labour market and are more likely to have some alternative means of support (e.g. their families) to fall back on.

5. Employment and output by sectors of the economy

Table 6 summarises the growth and percentage distribution of employment and output by industry groups. It indicates that agriculture is

Table 6. Percentage distribution and growth of employment and output by industry groups, 1972 and 1978

Industry group	Employment			Gross domestic product[1]		
	Percentage distribution		Average annual growth rate (%)	Percentage distribution		Average annual growth rate (%)
	1972	1978		1972	1978	
Productive sector	**52.9**	**52.8**	**1.9**	**44.5**	**41.7**	**−3.3**
1. Agriculture, forestry and fishing	32.5	35.9	3.6	7.2	9.0	1.5
2. Mining, quarrying and refining	1.1	0.8	−2.8	9.8	10.7	−0.8
3. Manufacture	12.7	11.1	−0.1	16.8	15.6	−3.4
4. Construction and installation	6.6	5.0	−2.8	10.7	6.4	−10.3
Services sector	**46.7**	**46.3**	**2.4**	**51.9**	**54.3**	**−3.0**
5. Transport, communications and public utilities[2]	4.1	4.4	2.9	6.1	7.5	1.2
6. Commerce[3]	13.2	13.0	1.8	33.3	28.9	−4.5
7. Public administration[4]	10.8	14.7	7.3	7.2	12.9	7.9
8. Other services[5]	18.6	14.2	−1.2	5.3	5.0	−3.4
Unspecified	**0.4**	**0.9**	**18.9**	**3.6**	**4.0**	**−0.8**
Total	**100.0**	**100.0**	**2.2**	**100.0**	**100.0**	**−3.2**

[1] At constant (1974) factor prices. GDP at constant (1974) prices declined from J$2,373.5 million in 1972 to J$1,953.3 million in 1978. [2] Corresponds to transport, storage, communications, electricity and water. [3] Includes distributive trade, insurance services, real estate and business services. [4] Producers of government (central and local) services. [5] Includes education, medical and health and professional services, personal services, non-profit institutions, recreation and entertainment, hotels, restaurants and clubs, and miscellaneous services.

Sources: Computed by the author from *The labour force, 1978*, op. cit., and Department of Statistics, Jamaica: *National income and product, 1978.*

the largest employer of labour. Employment in the manufacturing sector declined because of lack of foreign exchange, which made it difficult to obtain imported raw materials and capital goods. There was also a marked decline in employment in the construction sector as a result of the escalating costs of raw materials and the depressed state of the housing market.

In the case of "other services" the decline in employment is largely the result of the substantial decline in tourist receipts from J$108 million in 1972 to J$71 million in 1977. Significant increases occurred in public administration as a result of the emphasis on public sector activities, the expansion of the state bureaucracy and the increasing role of the State in the economic affairs of the country.

Table 7. Indices of employment, wages, prices, productivity and output, 1972-78 (1972 = 100)

Index	1972	1973	1974	1975	1976	1977	1978	Average annual growth rate (%)
Employment	100.0	100.8	105.3	110.9	110.0	113.3	113.8	2.2
Nominal wage rate [1]	100.0	124.8	150.3	175.5	186.0	195.1	231.1	14.2
Consumer price index (annual)	100.0	117.6	149.6	175.6	192.9	214.3	289.3	19.4
Real wage rate [2]	100.0	106.1	100.5	100.0	96.4	91.0	79.9	−3.7
Productivity	100.0	97.1	92.4	85.3	78.0	75.1	73.6	−5.0
Output	100.0	96.3	95.6	93.2	84.5	83.8	82.4	−3.2

[1] Nominal wage rate index $= \frac{\text{Index of compensation of employees} \times 100}{\text{Index of employment}}$.

[2] Real wage rate index $= \frac{\text{Nominal wage rate index} \times 100}{\text{Consumer price index}}$.

Source: Based on author's calculations.

6. Explanations for the level of unemployment

During the period under review real output (GDP) declined by 3.2 per cent a year; employment grew by 2.2 per cent annually and the nominal wage rate by 14.2 per cent; productivity declined by 5 per cent a year and real output per head of population fell by nearly 24 per cent between 1972 and 1978 (see table 7).

The poor performance of the economy is a result of not one but a combination of factors, for example the decline in capital formation, rising oil prices and world inflation, the introduction of an export tax on bauxite alumina which has affected its competitiveness on world markets, deficit financing, balance of payments difficulties, emigration of skilled workers, political and social tensions, and a general malaise in the society.

Relationship between employment and the real wage rate

As table 7 shows, real wages kept abreast of inflation up to 1975, after which they declined sharply. The decline in the real wage rate in 1978 is a result of devaluation, balance of payments difficulties, commodity shortages and shrinking output. The data also show that the index of real wages is higher than that of productivity, but there is no consistent pattern in the changes in the two indices. For example, between 1972 and 1976 the percentage changes in real wages were smaller than those in productivity; but between 1976 and 1978 the former declined faster than the latter. Economic theory tells us that there is an inverse relationship between employment *(N)* and the real wage rate *(W/P)*. The estimated relationship for the period 1972-78 is given by the following regression equation:

$$N_t = 156.9 - \underset{(-2.63)}{0.51} \, (W/P)_t \qquad R^2 = 0.58 \quad SE = 4.06$$

(The figure in brackets beneath the estimated coefficient is the estimated t statistic, R^2 is the coefficient of determination and SE the standard error of the regression coefficient.) The estimated coefficient is statistically significant at the 5 per cent level and it has the expected sign. However, the level of employment is influenced not only by variations in the real wage rate but by the elasticity of demand for labour with respect to the real wage rate. At the point of sample means the elasticity of N with respect to W/P is -0.41, which suggests that the demand for labour is inelastic.

Output and employment

The relationship between the level of output (Y) and employment is the following:

$$Y_t = 209.9 - \underset{(-4.39)}{1.11} \, N_t \qquad R^2 = 0.79 \quad SE = 3.53$$

It is generally expected that as employment increases output will also increase, but the empirical results indicate the contrary. The perverse relationship between employment and output may be due to a decline in productivity caused by employing additional labour whose marginal productivity is zero. The decline in productivity and real output may also result from the decline in capital formation, the lack of substitution between capital and labour, emigration of skilled workers, organisational structures, attitudes to work and the wave of industrial unrest that has characterised the labour scene since 1972.

Wages and prices

In considering policies and programmes to grapple with the unemployment problem it is necessary to bear in mind the relationship between changes in wages and price increases, since the well known Phillips-Lipsey hypothesis postulates that there is a trade-off between wage (or price) increases and the level of unemployment. The effect of changes in the wage rate on the price level is given by the following regression equation:

$$\frac{\Delta P}{P_{t-1}} = 0.82 + \underset{(1.59)}{0.75} \left[\frac{\Delta W}{W_{t-1}} \right] \qquad R^2 = 0.39 \quad SE = 8.51$$

where

$$\Delta P = P_t - P_{t-1} \quad \text{and} \quad \Delta W = W_t - W_{t-1}$$

The estimated coefficient of $\Delta W/W_{t-1}$ is positive, as expected, and significant at the 10 per cent level. It follows from the results that for each 1 per cent increase in the wage rate, prices could eventually rise by 1.33 per cent, and wages by an additional 0.58 per cent, which is a strong wage-price spiral mechanism in the economy.

7. Macro-economic policy proposals

Policies designed to alleviate the problem of unemployment and underemployment in Jamaica must be viewed within the framework of the over-all planning objectives and targets. Measures available to combat the unemployment problem include the following:

Exchange rate policy

The postwar economic policy of Jamaica has been based on import substitution industrialisation in the manufacturing sector. To support this policy there were low interest rates, exemptions of capital goods imports from customs duties, import quotas for manufactured goods, accelerated depreciation allowances and the provision of basic infrastructure facilities. Jefferson[7] noted that the import substitution industries operating under the Pioneer Industries (Encouragement) Law were not only capital-intensive in a country where capital is scarce, but failed to provide a sizeable boost to employment. Gafar[8] observed that the exchange rate was artificially kept overvalued and that the import substitution policy had the effect of subsidising capital, attracting resources away from industries that were potentially competitive given the economy's factor (labour) endowment, and distorting the allocative efficiency of the market. Little et al.[9] found that import substitution policies in developing countries led to a situation where agriculture (often a labour-intensive activity in developing countries) was subsidising manufacturing by 10 to 20 per cent or more of agricultural value added. Given the distortions in *w/r* (where *w* is the wage rate and *r* the rental rate per unit of capital) as a result of the import substitution policies, an overvalued exchange rate, the introduction of a minimum wage and the implicit tax on labour-intensive industries (e.g. agriculture), there is need to develop an exchange rate policy to reflect the true scarcity values of the factors of production in order to stimulate export growth, increase employment and maintain the balance of payments equilibrium.

In this context, devaluation has an important and dynamic role to play, since it can lead to reduced imports, lower export costs, an increased volume of exports, expanded production of local substitutes and hence employment growth. But this will depend on the wage-price spiral and the supply response of local production to relative price changes. As a policy tool, devaluation must be accompanied by other fiscal and monetary policies (e.g. reduction in the growth of money supply) to maintain internal and external balance. If wage increases have less effect than devaluation on the cost of living, devaluation may prove to be useful in reducing the level of unemployment. Alternatively, rather than adopting a policy of straightforward devaluation, a system of selective exchange rates (as for example the dual exchange rates used in many Latin American countries as an instrument of development policy) may be utilised to foster employment in industries that are labour-intensive (for example, agriculture and light manufacturing).

Agriculture, trade, and monetary and fiscal policies

Features characteristic of the Jamaican economy are the steady migration of population from rural to urban areas; the sluggish growth in agricultural output; the decline in the area under agricultural production from 1.9 million acres (770,000 hectares) in 1954 to 1.5 million acres (607,000 hectares) in 1968; the increased volume and value of agricultural imports (meat, cereals, vegetable oils, dairy products, animal feeds, etc.) and labour-intensive manufactures (textiles, footwear, light metal goods); and deficit financing and monetary expansion. There is need to take a careful look at trade policies, particularly tariff rates, which according to Lewis[10] are low when compared with other Third World countries. If conventional market forces prove ineffective to stimulate growth and regulate foreign trade, the theory of the second best suggests that tariffs or quotas or subsidies may well prove beneficial in stimulating local production of commodities hitherto imported, and hence lead to increased employment.

In order to stem the steady flow of labour from the rural to the urban areas, increasing emphasis must be placed on the role of agriculture in the total development process, since agriculture is the largest absorber of labour. A vigorous land reform programme should be implemented with the aim of intensifying land use both for crop and livestock production to meet local demand. Agricultural machinery, water pumps and farming implements should be granted import duty relief, and fertilisers should be subsidised to encourage farmers to adopt modern techniques of production. There should be farm support programmes, including a comprehensive scheme of agricultural price stabilisation and increased marketing facilities. Monetary policies and institutions should be developed to encourage an increase in the flow of credit from the banking system to agriculture, agro-based industries and other labour-intensive enterprises. However, in order to make agriculture attractive, emphasis has to be placed on the provision of adequate rural housing, infrastructure (roads, electricity supply and irrigation schemes) and other social facilities. But, in the context of the Jamaican economy, where agriculture employs about one-quarter of the labour force, this means that agricultural employment would have to grow by nearly 12 per cent yearly merely to absorb the natural increment of the labour force, which is growing at an annual rate of approximately 3 per cent. It follows that the encouragement of labour-intensive light manufactures and labour-intensive construction activities will not only add to total output, but reduce the level of unemployment.

Wage, price and incomes policy

On the basis of the empirical evidence we may safely conclude that there is a strong relationship between wages and prices. Wage increases can lead to inflation, with possible adverse effects on employment. Inflation in turn affects wage earners more seriously than profit earners or landlords. In view of the current high level of unemployment and inflation in Jamaica, some broad consensus should therefore be developed between the authorities, trade unions and entrepreneurs relating to price, wage and profit increases. The introduction of a universal minimum wage rate and the practice observed by Lewis[11] whereby the wage rate in high-productivity and high-profit sectors (bauxite and tourism) influences the rates in other sectors have had the effect of raising the price of labour, in most cases above the value of its marginal product, thus, paradoxically, accentuating the unemployment problem. (While it is true there is widespread poverty in the country, the price mechanism—the fixing of a minimum wage—should not be saddled with the function of solving the problems of income distribution and poverty. A tax-subsidy scheme, or training of the poor, creation of employment opportunities for the poor or a redirection of government expenditure to poorer areas are measures better suited to dealing with poverty and the distribution of incomes.) Unless there is some restraint on wages to guard against cost-push inflation, wage increases will nullify the benefits of comparative advantage associated with labour-intensive exports and accentuate the substitution of capital for labour. In short, a prices and incomes policy, in conjunction with exchange rate, fiscal and monetary policies, as well as good industrial practice, are suggested as the most promising means of grappling with the unemployment problem.

Notes

[1] I wish to thank Mr. Desmond Hunte, Senior Statistician, Central Statistical Office, Trinidad and Tobago, for his comments. All remaining errors and shortcomings are the responsibility of the author.

[2] From 1973 to 1977 the rate of exchange of the Jamaican dollar was J$1 = US$1.11; in 1978 it was J$1 = US$0.56.

[3] H. J. Bruton: "Economic development and labour use: a review", in E. O. Edwards (ed.): *Employment in developing countries* (New York, Columbia University Press, 1974).

[4] L. Squire: *Labour force, employment and labour markets in the course of economic development*, World Bank Staff Working Paper No. 336 (Washington, 1979)

[5] D. J. Harris: "Notes on the question of a national minimum wage for Jamaica", in Carl Stone and Aggrey Brown (eds.): *Essays on power and change in Jamaica* (Mona (Jamaica), University of the West Indies, 1976).

[6] T. M. A. Farrell: "The unemployment crisis in Trinidad and Tobago: its current dimensions and some projections to 1985", in *Social and Economic Studies* (Mona (Jamaica)), Vol. 27, pp. 117-132.

[7] Owen Jefferson: *The post-war economic development of Jamaica* (Jamaica, Institute of Social and Economic Research, University of the West Indies, 1972), pp. 141-147.

[8] J. Gafar: "An analysis of import substitution in a developing economy: the case of Jamaica", in *CSO Research Papers*, No. 10 (1979), pp. 33-50.

[9] Ian Little, Tibor Scitovsky and Maurice Scott: *Industry and trade in some developing countries. A comparative study* (London, Oxford University Press, 1970).

[10] W. A. Lewis: "Four steps to full employment", in C. M. Meier (ed.): *Leading issues in economic development* (London, Oxford University Press, 1976).

[11] Lewis, op. cit.

Bibliography

ILO publications

Conciliation and arbitration procedures in labour disputes. A comparative study. Geneva, 1980. x + 183 pp. Limp cover: 25 Swiss francs, ISBN 92-2-102339-7; hard cover: 35 Swiss francs, ISBN 92-2-102338-9.

The importance of effective systems of dispute settlement, adapted to suit the various national labour relations patterns, is widely accepted today. The absence of such a system can lead to widespread industrial conflict, with adverse effects on the community as a whole as well as on the relations between employers and workers and on the collective bargaining process itself. At the same time, the need to strike a balance between this need for effective dispute settlement machinery and the need for the bargaining parties to be free from outside intervention has been a central concern of labour policy in both industrialised and developing countries for the past three decades.

In this important study, which complements several comparative studies recently published by the ILO on collective bargaining systems and provides a background to the ILO's practical guides on conciliation and grievance arbitration (see *International Labour Review*, Feb. 1974, p. 185, and July-Aug. 1977, pp. 100-101), different national approaches to conciliation and arbitration in labour disputes are compared and guidance is offered on the development of various types of conciliation and arbitration procedure. This is the first full-length comparative study to have been devoted specifically to this subject by the ILO for nearly half a century.

Appropriate technology. Scope for co-operation among the countries of the West African Economic Community. Report of a study tour undertaken in Dakar, Nouakchott, Abidjan, Bamako, Niamey and Ouagadougou (11 November-10 December 1979), prepared by M. J. C. Woillet, ILO consultant. Geneva, 1980. ii + 104 pp. Tables, appendices, bibliography. 10 Swiss francs. ISBN 92-2-102359-1.

Research into appropriate technologies and their development, dissemination and application in the various sectors of the economy call for huge investments and skilled personnel that are not always available. It is important, therefore, to encourage regional co-operation so as to ensure that the limited resources available to governments are employed efficiently and effectively. The point of regional co-operation is to avoid the waste of effort caused by a duplication of pure and applied research activities and to create economies of scale both at the level of training and at that of production.

With a view to fostering regional co-operation among the countries of the West African Economic Community (CEAO), the ILO organised in 1979 a series of study tours with participants representing several institutions in the CEAO countries which are seeking to promote the use of appropriate technologies. The study tours concentrated on four issues of major importance for these countries: renewable energy resources; the processing of agricultural products; agricultural equipment and implements; and construction materials.

This report provides as complete a coverage as possible of the visits and discussions that took place during the study tours. It also contains a number of suggestions for promoting regional co-operation in the field of appropriate technology research.

Ergonomic principles in the design of hand tools. By T. M. Fraser. Occupational Safety and Health Series No. 44. Geneva, 1980. vii + 93 pp. Tables, figures, bibliography, appendix. 15 Swiss francs. ISBN 92-2-102356-7.

This penetrating and practical study is aimed at everyone concerned with the design, manufacture, purchase and use of basic hand tools, and especially at those in developing countries who are finding ergonomic information in this field hard to come by.

The first two chapters are devoted to the nature and historical evolution of, respectively, hand tools and the science of ergonomics. Chapter 3 examines the physiological and psychological aspects of human work, skill and fatigue. This in turn leads to a discussion of anthropometry and biomechanics in relation to tool design. Chapter 5 goes on to provide a practical guide to the human engineering of hand and small power tools, defining wherever possible the optimum design specifications for various classes of tool. A final chapter is given over to a discussion of design methodology, i.e. the principles of design a manufacturer should apply. An appendix lists the sizes, uses and other characteristics of many of the hand tools in common use.

Occupational exposure to airborne substances harmful to health. Geneva, 1980. viii + 44 pp. Appendices, index. 10 Swiss francs. ISBN 92-2-102442-3.

The protection of workers' health against hazards due to the contamination of air at the workplace, and the prevention of contamination of the working environment generally, should be the concern not only of those directly responsible for occupational safety and health but also of all those involved in the design, organisation and performance of work. The principles laid down in this new code of practice, which was adopted by a meeting of experts convened by the ILO with the participation of the WHO, are not intended as a substitute for existing national legislation, regulations or safety standards. They are intended rather to stimulate and provide guidance to governments, employers and workers, and are to be regarded as objectives that may be attained progressively in different countries and enterprises according to local circumstances and possibilities. The wording of the code is also sufficiently flexible to permit its adaptation in the light of technological progress.

Together with the code of practice on the protection of workers against noise and vibration in the working environment (see *International Labour Review*, July-Aug. 1977, p. 100), the new volume complements the Working Environment (Air Pollution, Noise and Vibration) Convention (No. 148) and Recommendation (No. 156) adopted by the Conference in 1977. A full glossary defines the terms used in the text.

Book notes

Abella, Manolo I. **Export of Filipino manpower.** Manila, Institute of Labor and Manpower Studies of the Ministry of Labor, 1979. v + 105 pp. Tables, appendix, bibliography.

This is a most useful and readable little book from the former Executive Director of the Philippine Institute of Labour and Manpower Studies, who is at present a staff member of the ILO Asian Regional Project for Strengthening Labour/Manpower Administration in Bangkok. He poses more questions on emigration policies in general and temporary contract labour movements in particular than one usually finds in the literature on the subject. He assesses the social costs and benefits of "exporting" Filipino workers, but is not content with merely *a priori* generalities: he estimates the actual amounts of dollars or pesos involved, making intelligent use of a limited data base. And he does not clothe his argument in esoteric jargon.

The issues raised in the first chapter, and given a forthright answer towards the end, revolve around the "two conflicting goals—maximising employment and guaranteeing protection—[which] are at the heart of the most important controversies in the field of manpower export and indeed in the whole area of employment policy". Assuming that the government adopts not merely a passive laissez-faire attitude but actively encourages temporary or permanent labour emigration, how far should it—or can it—go in licensing private recruitment agencies and ensuring decent wages and working conditions? This seemingly banal question is examined by Abella at some length with the help of the experience gained by the Philippine Ministry of Labour in suppressing illicit agencies, setting and enforcing minimum standards for wages and conditions, and dispatching labour attachés to countries with significant numbers of Filipino workers. The author states his own preference clearly: "A liberal attitude towards licensing new private recruiting agencies appears to be warranted as long as this policy is accompanied by heavy penalties for violation of the rules."

Abella's cost-benefit comparison for the country as a whole puts *(a)* increased income, *(b)* savings in capital that would be required to employ migrants if they stayed at home, and *(c)* acquisition of skills on one side of the balance sheet, and *(aa)* loss of output due to labour replacement problems, *(bb)* increased training expenditure and governmental overheads and *(cc)* inflation, loss of scarce skills and migration-induced capital intensity on the other. The scales, in this calculation, come down heavily on the positive side. However, it is as well to point out that *(c)* and *(cc)* are not quantified owing to lack of uncontroversial evidence and data; that remittance-fuelled inflation will surely arise through heightened demand for certain goods, land and equipment rather than, as Abella sees it, through expansion of the money supply; that output and training costs will be underestimated if profits are excluded from the calculation; and that there are other important factors on the debit side such as more conspicuous consumption, especially of foreign luxury goods. These criticisms may not change the cost-benefit picture dramatically. But the real problem is perhaps the cost-benefit approach as such, which favours a rigid framework at the expense of fresh and alternative ideas. One must credit the author with at least mentioning the problem, in the following words:

> For a developing country with still largely underdeveloped natural resources and where a majority of the rural communities are short of essential services in education, health, irrigation and other infrastructures, it is hard to find justification for a policy to export skilled or high-level manpower. The problem, however, is that such needs are not translated into effective demand because of a number of reasons, including the maldistribution of income.

In all, highly recommended reading for both administrators and researchers.

W. R. B.

Incomes Data Services Ltd. **Guide to pension schemes**. London, 1980. 90 pp. Figures, tables, appendices, bibliography, glossary, index.

A comprehensive and comprehensible guide to the labyrinth of the British pension system was long overdue. Incomes Data Services Ltd., an independent research centre in the United Kingdom that is concerned with various aspects of industrial relations, has at last succeeded in producing one. And most timely it is too, for whilst the principles of the system are reasonably straightforward, the structure and background of the state scheme and the occupational pension systems which reinforce it are complex. A bonus is that the text is noticeably free of the esoteric jargon which is all too often found in literature of this type.

The guide caters for a variety of needs. The newcomer to the British pension scene, for example, will find a brief review of the background to the system and its evolution, but it should prove equally useful to personnel managers or trade union officials who have to deal with pension matters in the context of employment conditions. Those directly concerned with the development and administration of occupational pension schemes will find that it deals with features of particular interest to them, notably the tax situation, the questions requiring consideration and to be asked of experts, the various options open and, of course, the arch-enemy, inflation and its consequences.

Nor does it ignore notorious problem areas such as the choice of financing system, the maintenance of purchasing power of pensions in payment, arrangements for those leaving the scheme, the increasing number of elderly persons, equality of treatment for men and women in terms of access, pensionable age and coverage, and the communication gap so often found when dealing with the workforce on the topic of pensions.

This is a guide which should be readily accessible to all concerned in any way with the introduction, development, administration and impact of occupational pension schemes in Britain.

M. H. J.

Jackson, Michael P., and Hanby, Victor J. B. **Work creation**. International experiences. Westmead (Hampshire), Saxon House, 1979. vii + 159 pp. Tables, appendices, notes. $20.50. ISBN 0-566-00287-6.

Millions of men and women are presently looking for a job in Western industrialised countries. Policy-makers are worried about the social and economic repercussions of rising unemployment, but inflation and concern for a sound balance of payments have so far restrained governments from making full use of demand-management tools like tax reduction, expansion of the money supply and other investment incentives which would boost aggregate demand and eventually result in increased employment. An alternative to waiting for these effects to work their way through the economy is for governments to attack unemployment directly, by giving subsidies to private firms or even by operating as the employer of last resort through public sector job creation programmes. Recently these instruments of public policy have attracted considerable interest because of their claimed potential to increase employment without exerting inflationary pressures.

This book is a collection of papers presented to the International Conference on Work Creation held at the University of Stirling in 1978. It is intended as an introduction to an increasingly important topic and hence does not cover *all* the employment-creating schemes that have been tried out in recent years; nor does it explore *all* the conceptual intricacies of programme evaluation, for which the interested reader would be advised to refer to the publications of the OECD's Manpower and Social Affairs Department.

Still, the book is a valuable guide to the subject. The emphasis is on programme description: seven papers deal with job creation schemes in the United Kingdom, Canada, the Federal Republic of Germany, the Netherlands and Sweden. But the remaining three venture on to more controversial ground: how do the cost effectiveness and the social utility of these schemes compare with those of other programmes? How should the target groups be defined? How can the success or failure of job creation schemes be measured? It is to the credit of the authors that these and other questions are raised (and some answered) in relatively untechnical language which makes the book accessible and interesting even to the non-expert.

B. B.

Leibenstein, Harvey. **Inflation, income distribution and X-efficiency theory**. London, Croom Helm; New York, Barnes and Noble Books, 1980. 122 pp. Figures, tables, index. ISBN 0-7099-0306-5 (Croom Helm); ISBN 0-06-494169-8 (Barnes and Noble).

This study is a think-piece on the relatively little explored subject of inflation and income distribution. Professor Leibenstein has written a number of works on micro-economics and development and recently published a book expounding his "X-efficiency" theory, which constitutes a radical departure from the conventional economist's preoccupation with maximisation. The present study was prepared for the ILO within the framework of its World Employment Programme.

After two introductory chapters the author sets out his theory of X-efficiency. Classical economic theory assumes that inputs are always optimally used so that, for example, output is maximal and/or costs minimal. X-efficiency theory, however, states that "the intervening element between labour time and actual output is basically a non-purchasable input that we refer to as motivation". Every job implies that the person "chooses the activities that he carries out, the pace at which he will carry them out, the quality at which they are carried out, and the time sequence of activities". X-efficiency measures the degree of ineffectiveness in the utilisation of inputs. Another part of the theory concerns the so-called "inert areas". An inert area is defined as "a subset of effort positions such that if a person chooses any one of these positions he has no inclination to move to any other position, despite the fact that there are different utility levels associated with different positions". According to this theory, "the size and nature of the inert area, compared to the impact of the inflation change, will determine to what extent initiatives are taken" for reviewing wage contracts (Chapter 4).

In general one can say (Chapter 5) that there are two categories of losers from inflation: "those whose income is derived from assets based on original cash valuations, and those whose bargaining power in the market from which they receive their income is relatively weak". In developing countries farmers, whose agricultural incomes are created outside the cash economy, have a hedge against inflation while the opposite is true for those who produce commodities subject to price controls. Additional factors which lead to increased inflation are discussed in Chapter 6. These are first of all related to the fact that employment contracts are "incomplete", so that a reduction in effort does not necessarily lead to a reduction in income. There is further the fact of economic life that cost increases do usually lead to higher prices but that cost reductions do not necessarily lead to lower prices.

Chapters 7 and 8 provide a new theoretical framework for analysing the causes and consequences of inflation. A large part of inflation, it is hypothesised, is due to the unequal bargaining power possessed by producers and consumers. Under current economic conditions it is mainly the producer that can determine price levels by fixing them on a take-it-or-leave-it basis. This reduces the pressure on the producer to increase the efficiency of his production process and enlarges his inert areas. The effect of inflation is likely to be highest on those groups whose bargaining power is low in the markets where they operate as a seller (labour market) and where they operate as a buyer (product market).

Chapter 9, which summarises the findings, stresses again that *a priori* it is not clear who is most vulnerable to inflation. Basically, this is an empirical question which has to be examined for each country and regularly reviewed. In addition to the direct effects of inflation described above, one should also examine the indirect effects. "In some cases", Professor Leibenstein points out, "the impact of inflation is likely to reduce the level of employment since inflation may stimulate investment in assets that operate as a hedge against inflation, without regard to the degree to which such assets are of an employment-creating nature."

All in all, one can say that this book contains a number of interesting ideas and theories about the direct and indirect relationships between inflation, income distribution and employment. It is now the task of empirical economists to quantify these relationships so that policy-makers can take the distributive consequences of inflation into account when arriving at their decisions.

W. van G.

Lewis, W. Arthur. **The evolution of the international economic order.** Princeton (New Jersey), Princeton University Press, 1978. 81 pp. Index. Paperback: $2.45, ISBN 0-691-00360-2; hardback: ISBN 0-691-04219-5.

This is an expanded version of two public lectures given by Professor Lewis at Princeton University in 1977. As the title indicates, the author's main concern here is not so much the current demand of the developing countries for a new international economic order as the way the existing one has come into being.

He begins with a perceptive historical retrospect, going back to 1850 and even further, in an attempt to explain the division of the world into countries exporting manufactures and countries exporting primary commodities. According to the author, the die was already cast in the first part of the nineteenth century when the Industrial Revolution failed to spread beyond Western Europe and North America. High agricultural productivity and a favourable investment climate allowed these countries to industrialise rapidly, whereas elsewhere agricultural productivity was too low to support the growth of an industrial sector, which was anyway actively discouraged by landowning interests. Under these circumstances, the latter countries had little option but to seize the "second best" opportunity offered by the Industrial Revolution, which was to export agricultural goods. In this way they began to participate in world commerce but it was the industrialised countries that dictated the terms of trade—naturally in their own favour.

The pattern of poor terms of trade for the developing countries has persisted over the years for a number of reasons. For a long time no major changes took place in domestic food production, and 60 per cent of the labour force was in low-productivity agriculture. As time went on, therefore, these countries became net importers of food, while matters relating to finance and trade in primary products were handled by foreigners or nationals pursuing their own private interests. This did nothing to assist the industrialisation process and, as a consequence, the domestic market for manufactured goods remained very limited.

Although this situation has improved somewhat during the past 20 years, since there is now a positive attitude towards industrialisation, the terms of trade are still unfavourable, having been severely affected by the sharp decline during the 1950s and 1960s in the prices of many products traditionally exported by the developing countries. Even today 50 per cent of the labour force in the Third World continues to be engaged in low-productivity agriculture, the access of these countries to long-term financing is rather restricted and most of them have accumulated enormous external debts.

What is needed to modify the existing international economic order, the author believes, is a revolution in the technology of food production in the developing countries. Any development strategy, he urges, should be based on the transformation of the food production sector which, in its turn, will create agricultural surpluses to feed the population and thereby provide the basis for industrial development. This has to be reinforced by adequate financing, which should be channelled mainly through the International Monetary Fund.

The present work constitutes a valuable source of information and stimulation not only for economists but for anyone interested in the origins of the current international economic order. Professor Lewis is always easy to follow and many readers will certainly endorse his thesis. However, the prospects for implementation of his recommendations remain highly uncertain, since to date one cannot point to any major improvements in the economic order. Indeed, the climate of confidence even seems to be deteriorating: at a recent conference held in Tanzania the International Monetary Fund was accused of imposing severe "monetarist" cuts on the developing countries, thereby depressing the general level of world trade and hindering the process of development in these countries.

C. S.

Lyon-Caen, Gérard and Antoine. **Droit social international et européen.** Paris, Dalloz, 5th edition, 1980. 423 pp. Bibliographical notes, index of judgments of the Court of Justice of the European Communities, alphabetical index.

This work, which is published as part of the *Précis Dalloz* collection, covers, as its title indicates, a wide field in which the main focus is on the social law of the European Communities.

International social law is discussed in a rather original fashion in three chapters: immigration and movements of manpower; trends towards the unification of social law (in which there is a fairly detailed examination of the standard-setting techniques and work of the ILO and the Council of Europe); finally, social law in international groups and multinational enterprises.

The social law of the European Communities is dealt with in a more conventional manner. After recalling the origins, general framework and development of European social law, the authors deal in turn with the free movement of workers, social security for migrant workers, employment and unemployment, the harmonisation of social policy and, finally, worker-management participation.

The importance and usefulness of this manual, which is mainly intended for law students, undoubtedly deserve to be brought to the attention of a wider public on the occasion of its fifth edition, which has been jointly prepared by Gérard Lyon-Caen, the well known author of the earlier editions, and Antoine Lyon-Caen, a professor at the University of Caen.

The principal new features of this edition are the detailed discussion of problems of private international law in individual and collective international labour relations (especially in the chapter devoted to international groups), and the account of further progress made towards social integration in the Communities, in which the case law of the Court of Justice of the European Communities occupies a major place. It was this Court which, in its interpretation of Regulation No. 52, laid the foundations for a sort of European social citizenship by replacing, in the field of social security, the notion of a migrant worker with that of a European worker who moves to another member country. As the authors point out, these developments should not disguise the difficulties arising from the sometimes divergent evolution of national social security concepts and systems. In this respect, moreover, the European experience undoubtedly assumes a more universal significance and value which, above and beyond the apparent diversity of the problems and situations dealt with, gives this study its unity and its coherence.

F. X. M.

Sojcher-Rousselle, Monique. **Droit de la sécurité et de la santé de l'homme au travail.** Collection "Droit social". Brussels, Bruylant, 1979. xii + 439 pp. Tables, bibliography, appendices, index of authors cited, alphabetical index. ISBN 2-8027-0224-6.

The emergence of what is already being called the post-industrial society has been accompanied by a considerable broadening and diversification of the aims of social policy.

For some years now a focus of concern in the industrialised countries—and one of the principal demands of the trade union movement—has been the humanisation of conditions of work. More recently attempts have been made to present the improvement of living conditions and working conditions as a single and inseparable activity.

In the field of occupational safety and health these aspirations found expression notably in the United Kingdom with the Robens Report (*Safety and health at work*, Report of the Committee, 1970-1972, Chairman: Lord Robens (London, HM Stationery Office, 1972)). The item "Safety and health and the working environment", which was the subject of a first discussion at the 66th Session of the International Labour Conference in June 1980, is a further illustration of this relatively new trend in worker protection policy: the aim being pursued here is to humanise the working environment by fixing fundamental objectives and defining the basic principles of a policy which will seek, in a coherent and structured fashion, to eliminate or control occupational hazards, improve the working environment and adapt work to man. Recent legislation (in the United Kingdom, France, Denmark, Norway, Sweden, etc.) also bears witness to a more reasoned approach to the problems of occupational safety and health.

Hitherto, however, the laws and regulations affording workers protection against occupational hazards have scarcely attracted the curiosity of jurists. These texts, which are essentially of a technical nature, are more often than not the work of labour inspectors, engineers, chemists, doctors and other safety and health specialists. The book by Monique Sojcher-Rousselle represents the first in-depth legal study in the French language of this vast and complex subject which the author has called "safety and health law for the working man", a subject which must be related to the more general field of the improvement of working conditions and is destined in her view to become a branch of social law in its own right.

The analysis of Belgian legislation in this study makes a valuable contribution to the ongoing debate about the organisation of prevention work and the responsibilities of the authorities, the employers and the workers in guarding against employment injuries.

In Belgium, as in other industrialised countries, the safety and health standards have their origin in the regulations governing dangerous, unhealthy or unpleasant work. These regulations, besides safeguarding public safety and health, made it possible to establish supervisory and control mechanisms which some people suspect of having been partly designed to accelerate the industrialisation process.

Through its analysis of the role of labour administration and more especially labour inspection in the protection and supervision of the environment and workers, and through its emphasis on the constant need for these state bodies to adopt compromises so as not to hold back economic development while at the same time protecting the workers' safety and health and maintaining employment, this work offers a novel interpretation of the history of industrial and post-industrial society.

The author also stresses the excessive degree of regulation instituted by the various provisions on employment injury prevention; this is not a phenomenon peculiar to Belgium and indeed more and more questions are being asked about the effectiveness of the system in various countries as well as at the international level.

These criticisms lead the author to look into the legal and institutional causes of the ineffectiveness of the legislation. Among these causes, the solution adopted at the end of the nineteenth century to the problem of compensation for employment injuries was decisive since the grant of automatic lump-sum indemnities, without investigation of the cause of the accident or disease, largely abstracted the phenomenon of occupational hazards from the moral implications and social censure which any prejudicial act entails. The result was that the prevention of employment injuries came to be regarded as an essentially technical question which failed to hold the jurists' attention, while those principally concerned, the employers and workers, shuffled off their responsibility on to the labour administration.

Questioning the traditional manner of organising prevention work, the author advocates diversifying the ways in which safety and health standards are introduced (in her view they could be incorporated more frequently in collective agreements) and, following the approach already adopted in the United Kingdom and the Scandinavian countries, examining prevention problems at the level of the undertakings themselves.

A major part of the study is devoted to identifying and discussing the basic principles of workers' safety and health legislation which are implicit in the regulations. The author would like to see these principles clearly stated in a law inspired by an innovative social philosophy, which in her view would undoubtedly be more effective than an accumulation of detailed technical standards accompanied by penalties which are rarely imposed.

In conclusion, the author considers that certain adjustments in the economic and social field could prove beneficial for workers' safety and health legislation. These adjustments, which relate to more qualitative criteria, are necessary to permit the industrialised countries to develop along new lines. Particular emphasis should be given to aspirations and achievements in respect of the humanisation of working conditions, the upgrading of manual work, the quality of life and participation. These themes are all bases on which to create in the coming years a new balance in the responsibilities of the authorities, the employers and the workers, a balance in which physical well-being, health, safety and even comfort at work would be of paramount importance.

With some 900 footnotes, which in themselves constitute a remarkably rich source of documentation, a comprehensive bibliography and several appendices illustrating the author's arguments, this work sets forth guidelines, offers solutions and puts forward concrete and coherent proposals. In adopting a critical and innovative approach to the study of the regulations governing workers' health protection, the book testifies, on the legal plane, to one of the major social changes of our time. It offers a valuable basis for thought and action to all those concerned with improving working conditions and the prevention of accidents and occupational diseases.

M. W.

VOLUME 119 — 1980

GENERAL INDEX

Page[1]

[1] Pp. **1-137:** No. 1, Jan.-Feb. 1980
139-270: No. 2, Mar.-Apr. 1980
271-405: No. 3, May-June 1980
407-530: No. 4, July-Aug. 1980
531-664: No. 5, Sep.-Oct. 1980
665-800: No. 6, Nov.-Dec. 1980

[1] Pp. **1-137:** No. 1, Jan.-Feb. 1980
139-270: No. 2, Mar.-Apr. 1980
271-405: No. 3, May-June 1980
407-530: No. 4, July-Aug. 1980
531-664: No. 5, Sep.-Oct. 1980
665-800: No. 6, Nov.-Dec. 1980

Page[1]

Bibliography

AUTHOR INDEX

[1] Pp. **1-137:** No. 1, Jan.-Feb. 1980
139-270: No. 2, Mar.-Apr. 1980
271-405: No. 3, May-June 1980
407-530: No. 4, July-Aug. 1980
531-664: No. 5, Sep.-Oct. 1980
665-800: No. 6, Nov.-Dec. 1980

COUNTRY INDEX[1]

[1] Pp. **1-137:** No. 1, Jan.-Feb. 1980
139-270: No. 2, Mar.-Apr. 1980
271-405: No. 3, May-June 1980
407-530: No. 4, July-Aug. 1980
531-664: No. 5, Sep.-Oct. 1980
665-800: No. 6, Nov.-Dec. 1980

---

[1] Pp. **1-137:** No. 1, Jan.-Feb. 1980
139-270: No. 2, Mar.-Apr. 1980
271-405: No. 3, May-June 1980
407-530: No. 4, July-Aug. 1980
531-664: No. 5, Sep.-Oct. 1980
665-800: No. 6, Nov.-Dec. 1980

KRAUS REPRINT
POSTFACH 15 11 09
8000 MÜNCHEN 15

In addition to special topically oriented issues, each publication of **IMR** contains original articles, documentation, legislative reports, extensive bibliographic services through book reviews, review of reviews, listing of new books and the International Newsletter on Migration (Research Committee on Migration, International Sociological Association).

VOLUME XIV NUMBER 4 WINTER 1980

ARTICLES

DOCUMENTATION